FOR YOUR
TOMORROW

The Way of
an Unlikely Soldier

—

MELANIE MURRAY

VINTAGE CANADA

VINTAGE CANADA EDITION, 2012

Copyright © 2011 Melanie Murray

Published in Canada by Vintage Canada, a division of Random House of
Canada Limited, Toronto, in 2012. Originally published in hardcover in
Canada by Random House Canada, a division of Random House of Canada
Limited, in 2011. Distributed by Random House of Canada Limited.

Vintage Canada with colophon is a registered trademark.

www.randomhouse.ca

Library and Archives Canada Cataloguing in Publication

Murray, Melanie Mae
For your tomorrow : the way of an unlikely soldier / Melanie Murray.

ISBN 978-0-307-35979-7

1. Francis, Jeff, 1970–2007. 2. Afghan War, 2001– –Participation, Canadian.
3. Canada. Canadian Armed Forces–Officers–Biography.
4. Afghan War, 2001– –Casualties–Canada. I. Title.

DS371.43.F73M87 2012   958.104'7092   C2010-907639-7

Text and cover design by CS Richardson

Printed and bound in the United States of America

2 4 6 8 9 7 5 3 1

Praise for *FOR YOUR TOMORROW*

"Melanie Murray sketches the life and tragic death of one Canadian soldier with such a tender regard for his motives that she allows us to comprehend the sacrifice without ever asking that we accept the war. . . . Through a sweep of history and myth—both personal and universal—she gives insight into a tragedy so many Canadian families have experienced. In the end, we come to share her family's understanding of Jeff's quest for higher purpose."   Carol Off

"Murray's powerful work contains the emotional resonance currently lacking in much of the writing about our involvement in the Afghan conflict. . . . Elegiac and lyrical. . . . A worthy volume not just for those searching for catharsis, but also for a nation looking to bear witness to the full measure of our soldiers' sacrifice."

Quill & Quire (starred review)

"An intimate portrait not just of Francis's life, but of his family and loved ones in the years leading up to his deployment and in the aftermath of his death."   CTV News

"A heartbreaking and harrowing account of war, *For Your Tomorrow* transcends the simplicity of usual conflict narratives. With clear-eyed but emotional engagement, Melanie Murray unearths the courage and savagery that define Afghanistan's and all wars."

Kevin Patterson, author of *Consumption*

To Jeff

11–11–70 | 04–07–07

Many serve and so few are recognized.

Lt-Gen (Retired) Roméo Dallaire

PROLOGUE

———

But who is set up for the impossible that is going
to happen? Who is set up for tragedy and the
incomprehensibility of suffering? Nobody.

Philip Roth, *American Pastoral*

JULY 1, 2007. The fireworks explode in a fountain of
light—flamingo, orange, purple, gold—and fade into the
darkness. They're cascading over Okanagan Lake, several kilometres away. But we can see them from the deck,
through the leafy branches of the walnut tree.

"Happy Canada Day!" I raise my glass to Mica sitting
across the table from me. She and her partner, Aaron, arrived in Kelowna yesterday, drove down from Yellowknife
after completing a three-year teaching stint at the First
Nations community of Rae-Edzo on Great Slave Lake. We
clink our glasses. "Ah . . . St. Hubertus Gewürztraminer. The
grapes grow on the hillside just a few kilometres from here,"
I say, swirling and sniffing, "lychee and melon on the nose."

"A hint of rose petal too," Mica laughs at our oenophile
charade, reminding me so much of her mother, my sister,
at thirty years old—dimpled chin, freckles, long dark hair.

"And here's to Jeff. To his safe return . . . in just a few weeks." She smiles, the diamond stud in her nose glinting in the candlelight. Her brother, Jeff, is serving in Afghanistan with the Canadian military. When I ask how she's coped with the anxiety of having her brother in a war zone for the past five months, she confesses her vulnerability. "I haven't told many people about him being in Afghanistan. On Easter Sunday, the day the six Canadian soldiers were killed, I really crumbled. We didn't hear their names for hours after it was first broadcast."

Three more soldiers killed just last week by another IED. I shake my head.

When Jeff was home for his mid-deployment leave in April, Mica got four days off and flew back to Halifax to be with him and their family. "He made us feel so confident about his safety," she says, her eyes brightening. "He said he'll be staying in the same secure outpost—they call 'the Hotel'—until he returns in mid-August."

The spicy scent of walnut leaves wafts in the warm breeze. We sip our wine and talk about their trip to Vancouver Island the day after tomorrow. They will meet up with friends to hike the West Coast Trail, one of the most gruelling treks in North America. For seventy-five kilometres, it follows a rugged shoreline of spectacular ocean vistas, tidal pools, marine caves and the tallest trees in Canada. Then they'll drive their packed-to-the rooftop black Hyundai back home to Nova Scotia.

Their camping gear clutters the lawn below the deck— tent, sleeping bags, foamies, head lamps, rain jackets, camp stove. Under the lights, Aaron attempts to organize it into their backpacks. "I don't know, Mica," he calls up, "either half of your clothes stay behind, or we won't be taking much food."

"We can eat salmonberries," she chuckles. "Melanie's been telling me that the bushes along the trail are full of them."

"Yeah, and we'll dig for clams, steam them over a driftwood fire—go native," he grins up at us. "No need to pack food."

Like two kids let loose for the summer, they exude the carefree excitement that comes with being on the road—your hours and days defined by a map of Canada spread out before you.

—

ON JULY 1, the sprawling military base at Kandahar Airfield morphs from a monotone of drab desert, brown buildings and tan tents. It flashes with red and white. Strings of Canadian flags decorate the railing around the boardwalk of the central square. Huge Canadian flags hang from the ceiling of the arena. In the Tim Hortons lineup, soldiers wear Canada Day T-shirts, red-and-white-striped hats, maple leaf ties and pins. Shouts and cheers ring across the square from games of volleyball, tug-of-war and water fights. The charcoal smoke of barbecuing hamburgers and hot dogs saturates the air.

For Jeff and his comrades, it's a welcome reprieve from five months of outpost isolation and on-call duty, 24/7. Each of them is allowed two pints of beer. Under the shade of a striped canvas awning, they clink their plastic glasses: "To Canada's one-hundred-and-fortieth birthday!" They drink to their country's contribution to stabilizing southern Afghanistan, the birthplace of the Taliban. A contribution with an enormous cost. In the past five months, sixteen of their comrades have been killed—thirteen by IEDs.

"And here's to the beginning of the end," Jeff says, smiling, "the last full month of our tour." They raise their glasses, savour every swallow of the cold amber ale—its hoppy aroma, foamy head, sweet malty taste and the lingering bitter finish.

A few days later, on July 4, the mid-morning sun blazes down on a convoy of armoured vehicles crossing a dusty desert road. Canadian and Afghan soldiers are returning to base at Sperwan Ghar, their early-morning operation completed.

In the gray light of dawn, they surrounded a Taliban IED cell, the bomb-making squad responsible for the deaths of three Canadians two weeks ago. A team of soldiers held the nearby mountain while their convoy rumbled up the road to the sleeping village, hoping to flush out the enemy. Forward Observation Officer Captain Jeff Francis was ready to call in fire support in case of an attack. The soldiers patrolled for hours through the sandy lanes and fallow fields. They knew they were being observed, but the Taliban remained in hiding. After a *shura* with the elders, the troops mounted their vehicles to head back to the base, tanks with mine-rollers leading the eighteen-vehicle convoy.

Now, in the commander's seat of his light armoured

vehicle (LAV), Major Chris Henderson mulls over the morning's operation. He expected the enemy to spring a trap. The locals had tipped off the Canadians to prepare for one. He knows the Taliban were there. *Why hadn't they shown their faces?* The convoy is following the same route they'd taken earlier that morning to reach the village, a road watched by tanks and military police during the soldiers' patrol. So IED threats are minimal, he reassures himself; an ambush is also unlikely on two infantry companies and a tank troop driving through open terrain. Still, he's uneasy.

Standing up through their swivelling turrets, gunners survey the brown lunar landscape and the distant barren hills for anything suspicious. They scan the road for signs of loosened gravel or wires snaking beneath the stones. They pass a field, lushly green with rows of two-metre-tall grapevines, alert to its hidden possibilities—ideal cover for insurgents, waiting in ambush or holding a remote control device connected to a roadside bomb.

A hundred and fifty metres from the road, a squat earthen hut sits within the maze of vines. It's normally used for turning green grapes into sweet raisins. But for the men in turbans, this grape-drying hut is a bunker. The ventilation slits in its metre-thick walls make perfect ports for firing and surveillance. The Taliban squad has been holed up here for days, the air rank with the smell of feces. They've been watching the road edging the field. It shows no evidence of their tampering. The mammoth cluster of Soviet tank mines and artillery shells was buried deep and long ago.

Between the rows of twisting vines, midway between the hut and the road, the dark-bearded Talib has complete cover. He grips a black plastic gadget in his sweaty palm—two buttons, two wires, a double-A battery. The convoy approaches. He lets the leopard tank roll by; he's waiting for the next vehicle, the sand-coloured RG-31 Nyala with a machine gun mounted on its roof. In the past few weeks, it has lived up to its reputation, one of the best anti-mine carriers in the world, and protected its crew during two IED strikes. It is a worthy opponent for their Goliath of a bomb. As the RG passes directly in front, he depresses the switch. Nothing happens. The vehicle's ECM (electronic counter measure) equipment jammed the signal from the detonator. But another RG follows in its dusty wake. His thumb hovers over the red button.

In the cramped interior of the second RG—a personnel carrier for Princess Patricia's Canadian Light Infantry—the men are buckled into narrow plastic seats. The uncomfortable seat belts are specially designed to prevent their helmeted heads from slamming into the metal ceiling should a blast occur. With sidewall armour plate and a steel-welded V-shaped hull, the twelve-ton RG is made to deflect blasts from below, to protect its occupants from the equivalent of two anti-tank mines detonating simultaneously. Encased in their steel womb, lulled by tires crunching over gravel, the men are at ease. Drained after four sweat-soaked hours of foot patrol, they're contemplating the lives they'll soon be resuming—just four more weeks.

The driver, Master Corporal Colin Bason, stares into the dust trail of the RG a hundred metres ahead. Clammy in his damp sand-coloured uniform, he longs for the temperate August heat of Burnaby, British Columbia—home—where he'll cradle his five-month-old daughter, Vienna, born just four days before he came here.

In the seat beside him, Captain Matt Dawe gazes dreamily out the tinted front window, envisioning his golden-haired boy, Lucas, blowing out two candles on his birthday cake. He remembers the rush of holding his firstborn child, two years ago on this day; wonders if Lucas will also become a soldier—like his father, uncles and grandfather before him. When he arrives back at the base, he'll call home, wish his son a happy birthday, tell him that Daddy will be home soon and bring his present.

In the back of the RG, Corporal Jordan Anderson, soothed by the drone of the engine, is half-asleep. He's imagining the celebrations when he gets back home to Iqaluit, just before his twenty-sixth birthday, and just in time for him and Amanda to celebrate their second wedding anniversary.

Corporal Cole Bartsch, in the gunner's seat, glimpses the gravelly desert through the slit of a window. He's reminded of home in northern Alberta. He can't wait to be back there, and drive his ATV into the prairie wilderness in August, to fish and camp without fear of rocket-propelled grenades, suicide bombers and IEDs.

The youngest of the crew, twenty-year-old Private Lane Watkins, pictures himself scooping up grounders at the field in Clearwater, Manitoba, with the baseball glove he's carried in his rucksack halfway around the world. He'll soon get to meet his three-month-old niece and namesake, Chloe Coleen Lane, named by his brother in honour of Lane's service to his country.

At age thirty-six the eldest of the crew, Captain Jeff Francis looks around, comparing the RG with the LAV he usually rides in with his forward observation team. It was a couple of kilometres away after the operation wound up, so he's caught a ride in Matt's vehicle. The windows are a bonus, he thinks, and it's the army's safest vehicle—but it's lacking the secure homey feeling of his LAV, *Lucky 13*. Through the narrow windows, the parched landscape rolls by. He daydreams about cool, clear water and August at Fanjoy's Point. He'll take his son, Ry—nine months old by then—to Grand Lake for the first time. They will sit on the sun-warmed slabs of southern New Brunswick sandstone, and Ry can kick his chubby legs in the water. When he talked with his mom there two days ago, she was repainting the bedroom, setting up a crib, getting everything ready for him, Ry and Sylvie to come to the cottage when he returns. Then they'll go to Malagash, to his granny's land on the Northumberland Strait. Ry can splash in the salty waves, dig his dimpled hands into the rippled sandbar.

Out the tinted window he glimpses a patch of green, an oasis-like relief from the monotony of desert brown. The verdant tangle of vines a satisfying sign of why he's here, of the life that's returning for the people—like Hamid, the Afghan interpreter dozing beside him, whose real name Jeff will never know. Working for "the infidels," this man risks the lives of his entire family. If he were killed, he'd be buried in an unmarked grave, and his family couldn't claim his body for fear of Taliban reprisal. And the soldiers of the Afghan National Army they've been mentoring these past months—comrades in this morning's operation—are men, like himself, determined to protect their families and live in peace.

Step by small step, he feels they're making a difference. Water is again sluicing through canals, irrigating this grape-field and bumper crops of melons and wheat. Fewer poppy fields mean less economic fuel for the Taliban's terroristic machine. Girls are entering schoolhouses. Boys are play-ing soccer again in fields the Taliban once used for stoning women. He'll soon be able to kick a soccer ball with his own son, dressed in the red-and-white soccer suit he bought for him in England, just before his deployment.

The thrill of fatherhood surges through him; a warm flush that has sustained him during stifling days and lonely nights; through slices of fear, and ramp ceremonies—his comrades' flag-draped coffins. He believes that the tomor-row of an Afghan child is inextricably linked to that of his own son's. Humanity, like terrorism, has no borders. *We are a spark beleaguered by darkness; this twinkle we make in a corner of emptiness*—a line from a poem, an English course at Carleton years ago, resurfaces in his memory. Sunlight beams through the emerald vines, shimmering like the poplar leaves outside his window when he awakens in the bunkhouse at Fanjoy's Point.

———

The seven men feel the earth quake beneath them.

A thunderous explosion splits the air.

The RG-31 Nyala launches thirty metres up into the dust and smoke-filled sky.

Seven bodies suspend in space. Seven spirits hover by the thin wall.

In the commander's hatch of the LAV fifty metres behind, Master Corporal Jason Francis is surveying the mud-brick barrier edging the vineyard, a young boy clambering along the top. A flash, as quick and sharp as lightning, pulls his eyes to the road ahead. A deafening boom muffles all sound for several seconds; then his ears are ringing as bullet-like pieces of rock ricochet off the LAV. A blast of fiery heat, the petroleum smell of cordite, as the gunner beside him bellows, "Contact!"

Sergeant Sean Connors hoists the hatch. A columnar cloud of smoke blackens the sky. "Ramp down, Mac!" he shouts. "Let's go, guys, move! Get the mine detectors!

Franny, call one-niner. Tell the major I'm on my way to the site."

He rounds the corner of his LAV. The RG's crew compartment lies upside down, leaning against a mud wall—wheels, axles, engine block blown off. He races to the vehicle. "Hey, is everyone okay?" he calls. "Hey! Hey!"

Not a movement through the splintered windows.

Not a sound from within the steel-encased tomb.

"I can't get inside," Sergeant Connors shouts. "Call for the medics. They might still have a chance."

———

In air acrid with smoke and diesel fumes, opaque with soot and powdery sand, combat engineers gape at the crater in the hard-packed gravel road—three metres wide, two metres deep. They shake their heads in disbelief.

Holy shit. That was one hell of a bomb.

I've never seen anything like it.

No vehicle could survive that.

Nor any body. The steel-armoured mine-resistant hull, the specially designed seat belts, the heavy helmets couldn't cushion the massive impact.

Seven spirits slip through the thin wall that's only and always a heartbeat away.

The explosion reverberates across Iran, Iraq and Syria; rumbles under the seas of the azure Mediterranean; resounds over the wind-blown deserts of North Africa; rolls over the waves of the blue-grey Atlantic, and crashes onto the rock-bound shores of southern Nova Scotia. On this hot July day in Eastern Passage, sunlight sparkles on windless water, wispy white feathers of clouds. In a beige, red-roofed, three-storey house overlooking the open ocean, a mother of a Canadian soldier has just made herself a sandwich. She's about to take her lunch out to eat on the sun-warmed deck when she's halted by the radio, the tones signalling the CBC hourly news. Conditioned in the past five months that her son has been in Afghanistan, she stiffens, her heartbeat quickens.

Six Canadian soldiers killed by an IED.

She puts the sandwich on the counter, her stomach knotted with fear.

She telephones CFB Shilo, her son's home base, and probes military officials for details. "We are unable to release any information at this time." A different response than the three previous calls that she's made after the deaths of Canadian soldiers have been reported—three times since February when her son began his tour of duty. *This could mean the soldiers are from Shilo.*

She waits for the two-o'clock news, paces back and forth, back and forth, in front of the picture window overlooking the main road and the ocean beyond. A car, dark blue, approaches. A flag flutters from its aerial—a red maple leaf on white, a Canadian flag. It passes her driveway . . . slows . . . turns around. She screams. Her high-pitched wail penetrates through the walls into the rooms of the neighbouring house, pierces the windows of the blue sedan pulling into her driveway.

Panting and sobbing, she runs to the phone.

In his fourth floor office at Canadian Blood Services in Halifax, the manager of field logistics, Russ Francis, has just slung his backpack over his shoulder. He's rushing off to a dentist's appointment, anticipating a brisk walk through the Public Gardens, a city block of flowers, fragrant with roses and magnolia on this hot afternoon. He doesn't drive his car to work; he prefers crossing the harbour on the passenger ferry, inhaling the bracing salt air. A walk is just what he needs right now to ease the anxiety curdling in his stomach. A colleague told him, half an hour ago, about the news report. *Good god—six more gone.* He's about to close his office door behind him when the phone rings. Should he answer it? He's running late. He glances at his watch, then back at the phone, ringing, pulling him back to grab it from its cradle.

"Come home!" Marion cries. "People in uniforms are getting out of a car. They're coming up the stairs." Her voice clotted with panic and horror.

"Oh my god," he says. "I'll have to get a drive. I'll be there as soon as I can."

Disaster has struck. He has to think, think logically. He can't feel, yet. He has to find their driver, Joanne. He has to get home and be with Marion. As he hangs up, a co-worker appears at his door with a sheaf of papers, a wide smile on her face.

"Lisa," he says, calmly. "I need to find Joanne. I need to get home. They just killed Jeff."

The driver manoeuvres the van through the tourist-crowded streets, speeds across the span of the Murray Mackay Bridge and down the busy four-lane highway. "Joanne, slow down," Russ says. "Getting there any quicker isn't going to change anything. Just get me home safely." He needs the time, the twenty-five minutes, to prepare for what he's about to face—to deal with the people who are there, to be strong for Marion. *Stay in control, be level-headed, work with the situation. Maybe he's wounded—not likely.*

Marion stands at the threshold, resolute: *I won't answer the door. If I don't answer the door it won't be possible.* A faint hope arises—*maybe he's only wounded.* She clutches the doorknob, buoyed by possibility. She bolts out the front door to meet three soldiers trudging up the stairs—the grim-faced messengers of Death.

———

"GET THOSE GUYS OUT of there! Get them off the ground!" I shouted at the radio when the news announced the deaths of six Canadian soldiers in Afghanistan. By 10 a.m., the identities of four of them were confirmed.

Now, waiting for the next report, I dwell in a limbo of fear, a refrain replaying in my mind: *this couldn't happen to Jeff . . . to my sister . . . we've already sacrificed one of our men, our father, to the maw of the military.* Faced with the randomness of roadside bombs, Jeff has survived so far. In only four weeks, he'll be home—home to begin a whole new phase of his life, as a father to his beautiful son, born just ten weeks before he left for Afghanistan. When he comes back in August, he'll be posted to Toronto, where Sylvie works for Air Canada. They'll begin their life together as a family. The map of his future is laid out, just waiting for him to return and step into it.

I try to stave off my trepidation, glad I have my packing to keep me occupied. On this sweltering July morning, I'm in a flurry of washing clothes and organizing suitcases for our trip to Halifax tomorrow. My younger son, Gabriel, and I will spend six weeks in the Maritimes, escape the motorized whirr of the Kelowna suburbs—the lawn mowers, weed whackers, leaf blowers, power washers, hedge trimmers; trade it all for the rushing waves of the

Northumberland Strait and the undulating call of the loons on Grand Lake.

Just before eleven, the phone rings. The voice on the line sounds at once familiar and strange. "Melanie, it's Russ," a timorous tone I've never heard from my gregarious brother-in-law. *Is something wrong? He must be calling about picking us up at the airport tomorrow.*

"Jeff was one of the soldiers killed this morning."

It's as if I've been jolted with thousands of volts of electrical current. Stunned and numbed, I can't move, or speak. *Not Jeff . . . please . . . not Jeff.*

"No!" I want him to take back the words. *This can't be possible.* In the background, I hear my sister moaning, keening for her son. I need to be there, to hold her.

A former military man himself, Russ can summon the focus of his logistician's mind, to override the turmoil of the distraught father. "Melanie," he says in a controlled, level voice, "do you know how we can get in touch with Mica?"

My god, dear Mica.

Today they begin their trek of the West Coast Trail. Once they're en route, they'll be in total isolation. But Mica said they would first have an orientation session at the trailhead. "Maybe we can reach them at the Parks office before they set out," I say, trying to reassure Russ. I know how much they need their daughter right now, their only living child. "I'll try to track her down."

I'm amazed at the clarity of mind that can surface in the turmoil of crisis, surely a survival mechanism. In my shaking and distress, I can find the phone book, locate the right section at the back—Government of Canada—and the Parks Department number; punch the digits into the phone, explain the urgency of contacting my niece, and finally reach the West Coast Trail Hiker Registration office at the Gordon River Trailhead. "Let's see . . . yeah, Mica Francis is registered to begin hiking today," says a pleasant voice. "In fact, she just had her orientation. She left about ten minutes ago to take the ferry to the trail."

"There's a family emergency. Mica has to call home as soon as possible." My tone is sufficiently panicked that a park warden is immediately dispatched to catch the boat before it leaves. "Please call me back to let me know if Mica gets this message," I say before hanging up. I imagine Mica, her dark hair tied back in a ponytail, her hazel eyes shining with excitement, sitting with her backpack in a boat on the edge of the Pacific, about to embark on an adventure.

———

THE MOTOR OF THE RED Zodiac idles loudly and waves plash against the gunwales. Mica can hardly hear Aaron talking to her from his seat on the other side of the boat. He glances up at someone approaching from behind her on the dock side, someone who says, "Is there a Mica Francis here?"

She turns around to see a woman in a brown Parks uniform. "That's me," Mica says, knowing even before the woman tells her, "There's been a phone call for you." She grips her heavy pack. "Oh no," she says to Aaron, "it's Jeff." They climb out of the boat onto the dock, get into the warden's car, and travel the kilometre back to the Parks office. Mica sits in the back so she won't have to talk. She wills herself to hold it together, attempts to hang on to a thread of hope—*maybe he's only injured.*

———

MY SIAMESE CROSS BATHES in a pool of sunlight on the birch floor. He licks his white paws, swabs his ears, licks and swabs, over and over—as if nothing has changed. I glare at the black phone, and visualize Mica making the call home. The dam of emotion bursts, releases a flood of tears and pent-up anger: "Jesus fucking Christ!" I scream into the indifferent air. "Why are they driving around in the desert when any second they could be blown up? It's a fucking game of Russian roulette!"

I respect my nephew's dedication to helping a suffering people, but I'm not a supporter of our military's mission in Afghanistan. Considering the country's thirty-year history of war, the corruption inherent in Afghan tribal politics, its police force and the government itself, I doubt that long-term progress is achievable. And with each Canadian soldier who's killed, I become more vehemently opposed to our military presence there. Most of the deaths are from roadside bombs. Why aren't helicopters being used to transport our troops? Is our military adequately equipped for combat? And now Jeff—my intelligent, brave and gentle nephew—has been struck down in the prime of his life, one more sacrifice to the god of war.

The ringing phone disrupts my crying rage. I seize the receiver, praying it's the hikers' registration office to tell me they've located my niece. But the lilting voice on the line is Mica's, higher pitched than usual, a voice that's trying to stay composed. She's not been told to call home, but to call me. The shock waves reverberate over the phone lines to an island on the edge of the Pacific. "Mica," I say, attempting equanimity, "you need to phone home right away."

"Is something wrong? Is it Jeff?"

"Mica . . . I don't want to tell you this."

"Is he dead?"

My lips move, but the words won't come out. Long seconds of silence before I can say, "Mica . . . I'm so sorry to have to tell you this. Yes."

"Oh god," she cries. "What happened?"

"A roadside bomb."

"Jeff," her voice trembles. "Just like the others."

"You'd better call home now, Mica. I'll be there soon."

"Okay, Melanie," she says, stifling her sobs, "thank you."

———

ATOP THE PEACE TOWER on Parliament Hill, a red-and-white flag flaps crisply against a clear cerulean sky. But in the offices of the Gothic Revival sandstone buildings, chaos reigns. It's one of the darkest days in the four-year Canadian military mission in Afghanistan, the worst since Easter Sunday. Just down the street on Colonel By Drive, in the concrete block towers of National Defence Headquarters, military officials issue press releases, determine next of kin, confirm phone numbers and addresses. They assign notification teams to knock on the doors of each of the six soldiers' families.

From coast to coast, in pods of three—a senior officer from the base, an assisting officer and a padre—they travel: to homes in Iqaluit, Nunavut; Burnaby, British Columbia; Whitecourt, Alberta; Clearwater, Manitoba; Ottawa and Kingston, Ontario; and Eastern Passage, Nova Scotia. They walk up to the doors of the parents who made him, nested and nurtured him until he could fly on his own; up to the doors of wives-in-waiting, each one crossing off the days on the calendar—*just four more weeks!*—until her beloved lies beside her in the long night; up to the doors of children who'll never again see their father's eyes beam love into theirs, never again snuggle into the shelter of his strong arms.

Sylvie and her mother drive through the maple-lined streets of suburban Ottawa, en route to see Sylvie's grandmother in her nursing home. Baby Ry snoozes in his car seat in the back. Sylvie is humming along to a song on the radio when the announcer interrupts: *This just in—six Canadian soldiers killed this morning in Afghanistan.* . . . Her heart starts thumping; blood rushes to her ears. "I'd know by now," she says, meeting her mom's eyes. "Jeff said, *If you hear it on the news, I'm fine.*"

But as they're parking the car, it hits her. She forgot to inform the Downsview Base in Toronto that she'd be away for a few days visiting her parents. A cloud of foreboding envelops her, casts its dark shadow on the sunny veranda where she sits with her grandmother, mother and baby son—four generations safely breathing together.

"I'm so anxious I feel like vomiting," Sylvie says as they're driving home two hours later. "I can't do this any more." Two days ago, she talked with Jeff for forty-five minutes, their longest phone conversation since he's been in Afghanistan. "I don't have a good feeling," she told him. "Something doesn't feel right. I'm nervous . . . maybe it's just getting too close to the end." He tried to reassure her with his mantric words: *I'm coming back. I'll be home soon.*

At four o'clock, they pull into the cedar-hedged drive-way. Flowering shrubs surround a two-storey red-brick house; a sentinel pine in the middle of the yard. The front door opens. Her father doesn't rush out to get Ry from his car seat as he normally does, happily lifting his grandson into his arms. He stays at the threshold, stares at Sylvie, and beckons with his hand for her to come into the house. She freezes. "What's Dad doing?" she asks her mother. Someone stands in the shadow behind her father. She unbuckles her seat belt and gets out of the car. She heads down the drive-way, away from the house, and steps into the street.

"Sylvie, come back," her mother shouts. But she walks on, hearing the panic in her mother's voice: "Sylvie, come back."

She stops, kneels on the hard pavement. Its heat and grit burn into her bare knees. "Mom, just give me a second," she calls back. "Just give me one . . . one . . . second." Every day that he's been gone she's wondered. *What would I do if a soldier came to my door?* Now, she knows. *Okay, they don't want to be here either. . . . Get up. . . . Get your ass in there . . . maybe he's only injured.*

She gazes back at the brick house. The house her parents brought her to when she was born, her childhood home. It could collapse any minute, she realizes. It's no different, after all, than the ones made of sticks, of straw.

———

JULY 6. In the murk of early morning, I lie in Jeff's bed, sleepless. Stars glow on the ceiling above me—the constellation of Scorpio—that Jeff put up there a couple of years ago.

One morning during the Christmas holidays, he came into the kitchen to show his mother the glow-in-the-dark stars he'd just bought. He stood on a bar stool and placed one large star over the wooden island where she was chopping vegetables. "This one's for you, Mom," he said. Then he went upstairs and positioned the stars on his bedroom ceiling: five stars in the outstretched claws; a string of six stars in the body; and five to form the smooth bend of the stinging tail—a horizontal outline of the letter J. He called down to his mother to come up and see his star chart. *A map, the place to find him.* "In one of the stars I shall be living," says the Little Prince in one of Jeff's favourite books—there on his bookshelf, an arm's length from the bed.

I arrived in Eastern Passage late last night. Marion and Russ were already in bed, exhausted from facing the impossible new reality of their lives, the details of their son's death springing up through the day like noxious weeds. When I stepped into Jeff's room, I was engulfed by his presence—but at the same time, confronted with his irrevocable absence. His khaki cargo pants hung limply on a hook behind the door. His framed photos looked at me from the top of the cherry-wood dresser: Jeff, a teenager, embraces his granny; Sylvie encircled by his arms, he in an orange polo shirt, she in an orange sweater—their first date, carving pumpkins; and the young man, a few months ago—a proud father holding his infant son. In the centre of the images, a brass statue of a seated Buddha; on the wall above, the framed World War II service certificate bearing his grandfather's picture.

Then my eyes moved to the titles in his overflowing bookcase. I shook my head, awed by the breadth, depth and eclecticism of his learning and intellect: several titles by his philosophical guru, Michel Foucault—*Society Must Be Defended; Ethics: Subjectivity and Truth; Discipline and Punish: The Birth of the Prison;* many on military history and strategy—Gwynne Dyer's *War* and *Ignorant Armies: Sliding into War in Iraq;* Michael Ignatieff's *Virtual War;* John Keegan's *A History of Warfare* and *Intelligence in War;* myriad martial arts titles—*Unleash the Warrior Within; Bushido: The Way of the Warrior; Budo Secrets: Teachings of the Martial Arts Masters;* numerous books on Buddhism—*Cittaviveka: Teachings from the Silent Mind; The Shambhala Guide to Aikido: the Way of Peace; Shambhala: the Sacred Path of the Warrior;* and two books by mythologist Joseph Campbell—*The Hero with a Thousand Faces* and *The Power of Myth.*

I pulled out Campbell's texts and flipped through their pages, replete with Jeff's annotations and yellow highlighting of passages:

The hero is someone who has given his life to something bigger than himself.

Freud, Jung, and their followers have demonstrated irrefutably, that the logic, the heroes, and the deeds of myth survive into modern times.

Herohood is pre-destined rather than simply achieved.

Was this another map, I wondered, another place to find him? During my flight from Kelowna to Halifax, suspended thirty-seven thousand feet in space, I had contemplated the arc of Jeff's life, its similarity to the archetypal stages of the hero's journey. A glimmer of light appeared, an inkling of a pattern in the events leading up to, and culminating on, July 4—events that otherwise seemed cruelly random and senseless: *Why Jeff? He had so much to live for.*

Now as I lie beneath his floral comforter, a salty breeze blows through the window looking east onto the ocean and the blinking lighthouse on Devil's Island. Waves hush on the shore—the sounds and scents of Nova Scotia, my heart's home. Every summer I leave behind the tropical dry heat of the Okanagan to dwell in the misty east coast and the warmth of my family. My sister Marion is as close to me as anyone can be. One year older, she was always there to play with, and watch over me, during our early childhood in Malagash. She's part of my earliest memory—when we were three and four years old.

Marion tells me where to get the matches: "They're in that wooden box on the coffee table. Make sure Mom's doing something in the kitchen.

Just take a few." When I get to the woodshed, she has newspaper crum-
pled on the floor. With the door closed, it's dark—a bit scary. But when
she scratches the match on the rock and puts it on the paper, everything
is illuminated—Marion's face aglow, her eyes fixed on tongues of fire
that soon ignite the dry wood chips littering the floor. Flames leap to
the wood stacked high around the walls. "Oh, oh," she says, grabs my
hand, and yanks me out the door. We run a few feet, then stop and turn
around, transfixed by the smoking crackling blaze.

Leo sisters, we celebrated our birthdays together over
campfires on the Northumberland shore; cut sticks from the
alders, whittled sharp ends, roasted wieners and toasted
marshmallows to charcoaled perfection. We dragged our
cardboard-box doll carriages down the dirt road to our
granny's house, and climbed the swaying silver maples,
daring each other to go higher and higher. Marion always
prevailed. She could skip with two feet when I could skip
with only one, and turn cartwheels across the lawn, her
coltish legs and black braids flying above her head.

Until our late teenage years, we shared a small bedroom under the sloping eaves of our storey-and-a-half house
in Oromocto and slept together in a saggy double bed. We
wore each other's clothes to school. A few days before I
was to graduate from high school, we buried our father.
Abruptly thrust from the kingdom of childhood, we spent
the following summer months visiting our grief-paralyzed
mother in the psychiatric ward of the Saint John Hospital.

Two years later, we each got married—within two
months of each other. In the early seventies, when I was

an undergraduate at the University of New Brunswick, Marion, Russ and three-year-old Jeff lived one floor below me in the Park Hill apartments overlooking the Saint John River. Some days, I'd hear a faint knocking, and unlock the door to see my freckle-faced nephew smiling up at me. He would toddle down the red-carpeted corridor to the stairwell, mount the cement stairs to the second floor, pull open the heavy fire-door and find my apartment—by himself. A few minutes later, I'd be opening the cookie tin when the phone would ring. *Is he there yet?* Marion would ask, and laugh with relief.

We both got degrees in English and in education, and became teachers—Marion in elementary schools in Winnipeg, Ottawa and Halifax, and I at a college in Kelowna. Like mirror images, we each had two children, and journeyed together along the rough road of motherhood. We shared its joys and challenges in letters, phone calls and summer visits, watching our babes morph into school-age kids . . . adolescents . . . adults. At the turn of the millennium, we buried our mother, and supported each other through the anguish that came with being orphans in our fifties. Last November, I joined in her exultation when her grandson—Jeff's son—was born, the primogeniture of our family's next generation. And in the past five months, I've commiserated in her all-consuming worry while Jeff was in Afghanistan.

Now, I must descend with her into the hell of our most fearful nightmare—one of our children dying before we do.

—

I wake to the smell of coffee, and a sound like the soft cooing of doves—the murmuring of a contented baby. I go downstairs to the kitchen. Marion stands in the sunlit window holding her grandson. For the first time, I see my sister as a grandmother, proudly embracing her treasure; and see her for the first time as a mother-in-mourning, grief already etching its fine lines in her face, darkly circling her eyes. And I behold for the very first time the bluest eyes, the rosiest chubby cheeks, the heart-shaped face and dimpled chin of Jeff's baby son, made in the image of his father.

I smile, for the blessing of this beautiful child; at the same time I cry, for his father's eternal absence and my sister's loss. I put my arms around them. "I am so broken . . . ," Marion whispers. We look into each other's eyes. I can feel it in her body, so fragile it could crumble in my arms. I hear it in her voice, cracked and dry. I see it in her brown eyes, brimming with tears. "How is this possible?" She shakes her head. "Before he left, I asked Jeff if he knew what it would do to us if anything happened to him."

"And what did he say?"

"He said nothing would happen to him—that he'd be okay."

Did he really believe this? Could he have gone *unless* he believed this? Jeff was no raw young recruit, harbouring youthful delusions of invulnerability. He joined the military at thirty after a decade of university studies. He embarked on the Afghanistan mission as a mature, thoughtful man. Was his response to his mother's question meant to quell her fears as he headed off to a war zone on the other side of the world? Was he, like all soldiers, playing the odds in God's lottery—that significantly more would survive than be killed, that he wouldn't be one of the unlucky ones?

Before he left for Afghanistan, Jeff must have looked death in the face. Forty-two of his comrades had already been killed—one a friend from his regiment, Nichola Goddard, also a forward observation officer. Like every deployed soldier, Jeff had to ensure that his legal affairs were in order, had to choose a photograph to be issued to the media in the event of his death. He posed in his dark green uniform in front of the Canadian flag, knowing there would only be one reason that his family would ever see this picture—enlarged to a 24-by-36-inch framed colour portrait and delivered to his grief-stricken family. When you see these photos of our soldiers in the media, you'll notice that none of them are smiling.

This picture isn't the one Jeff chose to be released in the event of his death. Rather, he selected one taken in Afghanistan: He stands in front of his crew's LAV—*Lucky 13*—dressed in his tan camouflage uniform and helmet with dust goggles attached. The desert sun lights up his face, the boyish freckles on his sunburnt nose and cheeks. His hazel eyes squint, but his gaze is direct. And he is smiling, a knowing half-smile. It's a photo that seems to say *amor fati,* love of one's fate—not fatalism—but love of the life one is called to live.

I. BIRTH

—

Our birth is but a sleep and a forgetting:
The Soul that rises with us, our life's Star,
Hath had elsewhere its setting,
And cometh from afar:
Not in entire forgetfulness,
And not in utter nakedness,
But trailing clouds of glory do we come . . .

William Wordsworth, "Ode: Intimations of
Immortality from Recollections of Early Childhood"

NOVEMBER 11, 1970

On a grey November morning, the smell of snow in the air, a young man and woman will soon cross a threshold. They will enter a three-storey yellow brick building. A hospital, built high on a hill, overlooks a town nestled between two rivers, the meandering Oromocto—which gives the town its Aboriginal Maliseet name—and the mighty Saint John, which flows hundreds of kilometres southeast to the Bay of Fundy. The man carries a small white suitcase and a large shoulder bag, a red corduroy bag packed with flannelette diapers and blankets, tiny nighties, terry-cloth sleepers, hand-knit woollen sweaters, bonnets and booties. With his other hand, he opens the door wide for his young wife. She catches a glimpse of her round silhouette mirrored in the glass door. *I'll be casting a different reflection the next time I pass this way,* she thinks, feeling her belly silently quaking.

Settled into the hospital bed, her long dark hair fanned out on the white pillow, Marion hears the skirl of bagpipes drifting up the hill from the cenotaph—a pibroch so familiar she can sing along in her mind:

> There was a soldier, a Scottish soldier,
> Who wandered far away and soldiered far away,
> There was none bolder, with good broad shoulder . . .

Between contractions, that rush in gentle waves every ten minutes, she envisions the slope above the river, the piper in a red-green tartan kilt; wreaths studded with poppies; a grey granite monument engraved with the names of fallen soldiers. A Canadian flag flaps in the wind; wires clink against the steel pole. Grey-haired war vets in navy berets and blazers, with gleaming medals, stand in solemn salute.

"The Last Post," the bugler's call, echoes through the hospital window: *They shall not grow old, as we that are left grow old.* "The last time I went to the cenotaph," she tells Russ, sitting in the armchair beside the bed, "was with Dad—three years ago, I think. We walked together down the hill to the ceremony. It must have been a Saturday, or he'd have been in a parade himself on the base."

Father and teenage daughter crossed the stubbly school

field behind their house, the wind whirling yellow leaves around their legs. She wanted to ask him about his war—the Second World War, she'd read about in history class. But he never talked about it. He was a man of few words; spoke more with his wide hazel eyes and his flashing grin. Only once when she was a child, thought to be asleep upstairs, she'd overheard him tell his brother about his platoon entering a village in Holland: "Bullets started flying—zinging over my head, coming from every direction . . . I've never been so scared in my life." Maybe he told his stories to his buddies at the Malagash Legion or at the Sergeants' Mess happy hour, exorcised his demons over one too many pints of Moosehead.

He had survived that day in Holland, and that war. He'd survived to become her father four years later, but not long enough to become a grandfather to the child about to be born. That day they strolled together to the cenotaph was his last Remembrance Day ceremony. The following year he was in Cyprus, wearing the blue beret of the United Nations Peacekeeping Force. And the spring after that—when he was forty-five years old—"The Last Post" sounded at his funeral. Sergeant Clifford Murray's final duty concluded.

Water gushes between her legs. Her baby awakens from its sleepy sojourn, and commences its first dangerous journey, moving down the constricted canal of birth. Through the long afternoon, the waves of contractions mount into tsunamis that pull her under into dark swirling currents; until they finally break, leave her breathless and panting in their wake. She resurfaces to the squeeze of a moist hand on hers, opens her eyes to glaring fluorescent lights and Russ's face, smiling uneasily. Daylight wanes and night comes on—a Herculean twelve-hour labour—until she feels the head, bears down and pushes out the crown of damp dark hair. The doctor's gloved hands ease out the broad shoulders, first one, then the other. At 8:38 p.m., a blood- and mucus-coated body slips through the narrow opening into the world. A bleating cry, then the words her family has been hoping for nine months to hear: "It's a boy!"

She cradles the miracle of his nine-pound body next to her, strokes the velvety pink fingers curled against his cheek. She is struck by the weight of this tiny being, the weight of responsibility she now carries—his life has come from her; his survival depends on her. *So this is what it means to be a mother.* Since that early spring annunciation—the crocuses just sprouting in the gardens—when she walked into the doctor's office a twenty-year-old maid, and walked out in a haze of uncertainty—a mother to be—she has wondered how she would feel, if *she* would be any different.

Marion cuddles her infant son closer. She gazes into his bleary blue eyes, at the cleft in his chin, and calls him by his name—Jefferson Clifford.

> Our first homes are within the bodies of women.
> These are the homes that precede nations
> and from which nations may emerge.
> Nations are born from the blood and water and babies
> that emerge from between the thighs of women.
>
> Katherine G. Sutherland, "Land of Their Graves"

———

WHAT ARE THE ODDS that the bagpipes that heralded Jeff's birth would be from the same regiment—the Second Battalion, Royal Canadian Regiment—that he would support to his death thirty-six years later? The piper calling from the cenotaph, as Jeff initiated his passage into the world, was like the herald in so many myths. A figure or divine sign summons heroes to their destiny: a burning bush startled young Moses so God could invoke him to lead the Israelites from Egypt; a blaze of light and unseen voices told fourteen-year-old Joan of Arc that she was to be the saviour of France. Just as the bagpipes harbingered Jeff's birth and his destiny on 11-11-70, they would also accompany the ceremonies that honoured his death and his return to the earth on 17-07-07. "The herald's summons may be to live," Joseph Campbell writes, "or at a later moment of the biography, to die." Every year on Jeff's birthday, Remembrance Day, the pipes resound at cenotaphs around the world and at his gravesite overlooking the sea.

Their wild notes also evoke the days of clan warfare in the Scottish Highlands where our family has deep ancestral roots. The chieftain's hereditary piper rallied the troops with his *piob mhor*—the great Highland bagpipe. He sounded the clan song, led the men onto the battlefield and played for as long as he could stand. The pipes' penetrating wail carried for miles, rising above the roar of the battle. During the Highland uprisings of the 1700s, the kilted northern "savages" with their Gaelic war songs so cowed the English troops that the British government classified the bagpipes as an instrument of war. A set of pipes attached to a sheep's stomach became such a powerful symbol of Scottish cultural integrity and resistance that for over forty years playing the bagpipes or wearing "the plaid" was a punishable crime. The 1747 Act of Proscription decreed six months' imprisonment for the first offence; for the second, exile—*to any of His Majesty's plantations beyond the Seas.*

Highlanders integrated into the British Empire's Scottish regiments—the Scots Guards and the Black Watch—and brought their pipes with them. Jeff's more recent forefathers also rallied to the bagpipes during the First and Second World Wars as pipers continued the tradition of leading troops into combat. Jeff's maternal and paternal grandfathers, his great-grandfathers and great-uncles all marched to the pipes and drums of "The Highland Laddie," the regimental march-past of the Cape Breton Highlanders:

On his head a bonnet blue
Bonnie laddie, Hielan' laddie
Tartan plaid and Hielan' trews
Bonnie laddie, Hielan' laddie.

Jeff himself hearkened to their call during pre-deployment training exercises at CFB Wainwright, Alberta. "Scotland the Brave" roused the troops on the Canadian prairie for the coming mission in a land as remote, desolate and feudal as the Scottish Highlands three centuries ago. And since the bagpipes also have a lengthy history of escorting fallen warriors to their graves, Jeff heard their laments in the Afghan desert; a lone piper knelling "Amazing Grace" as his comrades' flag-draped caskets traversed the Kandahar Airfield. The opening line—*Amazing grace, how sweet the sound*—now seems bitterly ironic, a refrain synonymous with loss and suffering.

———

I HAD ALWAYS SENSED that the day of my nephew's birth—Remembrance Day—was a sign: this first child of our family's next generation proclaimed "in remembrance" of our father. Jefferson Clifford carried on my father's spirit as well as his name. His birth meant rebirth and continuance: phoenix-like, new life emerged out of the ashes. That Jeff would develop into a man so much like my father—in his reticent personality and gentle demeanour—was yet to be seen. In a 1996 letter, Jeff's grandmother wrote to him, "You are my little Clifford—your Grandfather Murray is so much closer to all of us because we have you. You brought so many happy times to me back then when I needed so much. You are so much like your Grandfather Clifford in your ways and looks, and I'm so proud you're like him."

Now, in light of Jeff's calling and the cause for which he died, his birth date resonates with numinous undertones. Born on the day that honours the wartime sacrifices of soldiers and civilians, he is one of those soldiers now remembered on this day for his sacrificial death. Moreover,

November 11 is St. Martin's Day, the feast day of the patron saint of soldiers. A fourth-century martyr, Martin was born in what is now Hungary. He was named after Mars, the Roman god of war, but was reluctant to become a soldier like his father. At the age of ten, Martin secretly attended the local Christian church, a new sect that his parents distrusted. He longed to become a Christian monk, but was forced to join the army when he was fifteen. It was while he was a soldier, however, that Martin experienced the vision that would become his defining legend.

One frosty November day, eighteen-year-old Martin was on garrison duty in Amiens, France. Dressed in his officer's armour and a white lamb's-wool cloak, he was riding through the crowded city gates when he noticed a beggar in rags, trembling from the cold. Martin reined in his horse and removed his cloak. He slashed it in two with his sword and handed half of it to the beggar. Heading back to barracks that afternoon, Martin came upon another beggar shivering by the roadside. Again, he stopped, took off the remaining half of his cloak, and offered it to the man. As Martin resumed his journey, facing a long ride in freezing temperatures, the sun burst through the grey snow clouds and the frost began to melt.

That night, Martin dreamed he saw Jesus wearing half of his lamb's-wool cloak. "Here is Martin, the Roman soldier who has clad me," Jesus said to the angels encircling him. This dream set the course for Martin's life of piety. He was soon baptized. Eventually he became Bishop of the Abbey of Tours in France. Martin performed many miracles

throughout his long life, but it was his humility and be-
nevolence that made him legendary. He was buried, at his
request, in the cemetery of the poor on November 11. The
phenomenon of a sunny break on a gloomy November 11
is still called Verao do Sao Martino, Portuguese for "St.
Martin's Summer."

That the patron saint of soldiers is a man celebrated for
his compassion and humbleness belies the soldier stereo-
types in popular culture—the macho GI Joe, Rambo or
Arnold Schwarzenegger characters who glorify violence
and killing as a legitimate means to an end. Real-life soldiers are often propelled by the altruism embodied in their
patron saint, motivated by love more than hate—love of
country, of humankind, of freedom. St. Martin personi-
fies the humanitarian ethics that guide many soldiers—the
ideals that would one day inspire the baby born on his Feast
Day in 1970.

————

THE CONSTELLATION OF SCORPIO glows on the ceiling
of Jeff's bedroom. As I lay in his bed the night after his
death gazing up at those stars, I wondered why he needed
to put them up there. Why did he place that star above his
mother's head in the kitchen? *In one of those stars I shall be
living.* Many philosophers have speculated about the connection of heavenly bodies to an individual's destiny. "Every
human being has his star," wrote the Austrian anthroposo-
phist Rudolf Steiner, "which determines what he works on

between death and a new birth, and he comes from the particular direction of a particular star."

Goethe went so far as to say that he waited in the womb for the auspicious hour of the constellation under which he wanted to enter the world:

> On the 28th of August, 1749, at mid-day, as the clock struck twelve, I came into the world at Frankfort-on-the-main. My horoscope was propitious. The sun stood in the sign of the Virgin and had culminated for the day; Jupiter and Venus looked on this with a friendly eye, and Mercury not adversely; while Saturn and Mars kept themselves indifferent; the Moon alone, just full, extended the power of her reflection all the more as she had then reached her planetary hour. She opposed herself, therefore, to my birth, which could not be accomplished until this hour was passed.

Jeff's birth under a constellation ruled by Mars, the eponymous planet of the Roman god of war, seems like one more synchronous piece of the puzzle of his destiny. The red and fiery planet of Mars signifies aspiration, striving, giving everything to realize one's longings and desires, no matter what the risk—all traits that would define Jeff's character. The moon enters Scorpio midway through autumn when the wind strips yellowing leaves from the trees, and nature appears to die as it prepares for renewal. "Scorpio is the love song on the battlefield and the war cry on the fields of love," write Chevalier and Gheerbrant, "the

Scorpio-type a bird which can only confidently stretch its wings in the midst of gales, its temperament being storm and its environment tragedy."

I wonder too if Jeff's inevitable impulse to become a soldier could have been encoded in his genes, stirring in his solid infant body from the moment of his birth. Does our ancestry live in us and shape us in ways beyond our conscious awareness? Generations of marching men form his ancestral past. His father, Major Russell Francis, served in all three branches of the military—army, navy and air force—for thirty years. Jeff's paternal grandfather enlisted at eighteen to fight with Cape Breton's North Shore Infantry Regiment in World War II, then soldiered for another twenty-five years. But Jeff's most compelling ancestral role model was the grandfather he never knew.

A nineteen-year-old farm lad from Tatamagouche Mountain in Nova Scotia, Angus Clifford Murray enlisted in 1942 with the Cape Breton Highlanders. His wood-framed World War II Service Certificate always hung above the brown tweed rocking chair in my grandmother's dining room: faded pictures of the king and queen at the top, crests of the nine provinces around the border; above the Nova Scotia crest, a black-and-white photo of my handsome young father, sculpted cheekbones and dimpled chin. His carefree smile and the roguish tilt of his beret seemed to belie the seriousness of his profession.

The dining room's hardwood floor was scattered with colourful rugs my grandmother had hooked over the years from remnants of old clothes. Some had khaki wool backgrounds from my great-uncles' World War I uniforms. As a child, I noticed how my grandmother's eyes would linger on my father's war certificate, and thought she must have been proud of her son's service overseas. But perhaps that reflective gaze was one of relief, of gratitude, that he'd come home— all his limbs intact, unlike so many thousands of young men. Weaving details I'd collected from family stories, I created a picture of the day my father departed for the war. He rose at four in the morning to hitchhike to Truro where he would catch the train that would take him to Halifax. No one but his twin sister, Pearl, got up to say goodbye.

Sometimes I'd sit in the rocking chair scrutinizing my father's picture, imagining him that morning in early spring. *In the dawning light, he strolls down the lane with his rucksack on his back. He turns around to take one long last look at the red farmhouse where he was born; the weathered grey barns where he milked cows since he was five years old; the greening fields he ploughed with a team of horses since he was nine. Then he heads down the dirt road that will take him to the crossroads, to his first trip on a train, his first voyage over the ocean on a ship that will carry him to the war.*

In becoming soldiers, both my father and Jeff perpetuated a warrior tradition rooted in our Gaelic family tree. Our earliest known ancestor, the Flemish knight Freskin de Moravia, was the progenitor of the Murrays of Tullibardine and the Dukes of Atholl. To this day, from his thirteenth-century castle at Blair Atholl in Perthshire, the Duke of Atholl maintains the only legal private army in the United

Kingdom, the Atholl Highlanders. But the opulence of Blair Castle—its grand portrait hall, drawing rooms with red damask wall coverings and massive oak bookcases, finely carved staircases and marble chimney pieces—was many worlds away from the raw northern Highlands where my crofter ancestors struggled to survive.

My father's grandfather and namesake, Angus Murray, descended from Sutherlandshire clans who farmed the crofts in Rogart as far back as there is record. But their indigenous connection to the land was abruptly severed in the early nineteenth century. The British Duke of Sutherland evicted thousands of tenants from his million-acre estate to earn a more lucrative income from *caorach mhòr,* the big black-faced sheep from southern Scotland. *An Diùc Dubh,* the Black Duke, deracinated the crofters like bothersome weeds and razed their houses to the ground; the Sutherland skies stained blood red with blazing *clachans*. His one-hundred-foot sandstone statue, erected in 1834, still peers down from the summit of Ben Bhraggie. "Its back to the glens he emptied," writes John Prebble in *The Highland Clearances.* "It faces the sea to which his policies committed five thousand people as emigrants or herring-fishers."

The flood of propaganda about Canadian immigration promised my displaced forebears an escape from poverty and the opportunity to own two hundred acres of land. Desperate to restore their uprooted lives, my Murray, Sutherland, MacIntosh and MacLean ancestors bade farewell to Sutherland's heather-covered moors and glens, its lochs and braes and bens—the landscape imprinted on their

Gaelic souls for generations. *Cha till mi tuille*—"We shall return no more."

In May 1803, Alexander and Margaret Murray, their daughter Christy and her husband, William MacIntosh, packed their bundles with oatcakes and water. They trudged ten miles over moors abloom with golden gorse to Golspie on the northeast coast. At the Littleferry pier—a port-of-sailing advertised by some unscrupulous emigration agent—they were herded onto the *Perseverance* as steerage passengers, crammed into a dank cavern below the deck. Without portholes or ventilation, the overcrowded hold soon reeked of unwashed bodies, urine and vomit. They tossed across the stormy Atlantic—survived hunger, sea-sickness, dysentery, smallpox, cholera—and six weeks later, sailed into Pictou Harbour, New Scotland. They gaped at the jungle of evergreens skirting the shore and at the buckskin-clad Mi'kmaq watching through the trees.

The most accessible shore lands and river valleys had already been taken up by settlers and land speculators. So they travelled inland to the Cobequid Mountains in north Colchester County, remote and rugged like their Highland hills, but dark with impenetrable forests. Christy and William's daughter, Annie, married another Rogart emigrant, Angus Sutherland—nicknamed "Prince" as he so resembled Bonnie Prince Charlie—his red hair, high cheek-bones and heart-shaped face. Early one spring morning in 1813, twenty-two-year-old Angus set out to find the tract of land described on his ticket of location from the Philadelphia Land Company: *five miles east of the West Branch settlement.*

With no road to follow, only a trail marked by blazes—chips cut into the trees at eye level—Angus used the position of the sun, the contours of the ridges and the location of streams to guide him through the gloomy forest, two-hundred-foot pines blocking the sunlight. Raised on the barren coast of northeast Sutherland, Angus flinched at the unnerving sounds. Trunks and branches cracked in the wind like gunshots. Unknown animals darted through the under-brush, entangled with deadfalls. He tromped and bush-whacked all day, breathing the pungent odour of spruce and fir. As daylight waned, he spied an east-west baseline of blazes cut a mile long—the boundary of his land. He searched out a source of water and found a brook bubbling at the foot of a ravine. He sank to his knees and drank from the stream, as cold and fresh as a Rogart burn, cupped the icy water over his face and head. He had arrived.

Angus and Annie hewed the primeval evergreens from their land. They built a rock foundation and erected a log house. They cleared fields for farming, fashioned stone fences and planted apple trees. They raised four sons and four daughters on the farm that became known as "the Hennie-Prince farm." The six-mile trail that Angus hacked through the timbered mountains from the West Branch to his land grant eventually became the established route to the settlement known as Earltown. Over the years, the footpath was widened for horses, carriages and sleighs. In the twentieth century, it was gravelled, then straightened and paved. Highway 256, which we drive on today, still follows the trail cut by Angus, my great-great-great grandfather.

Inured to isolation and poverty in the land they'd left, my ancestors adapted to the hardships of pioneer life, coaxing crops to grow in the shallow soil of the Earltown hills. "Highlanders of the humblest class," Catharine Parr Traill wrote in her pioneer memoir *The Backwoods of Canada,* form "the class of people to whom this land is so admirably adapted . . . the unlettered and industrious labourers and artisans."

A weather-beaten region open to the sea on three sides, the Scottish Highlands were still a world apart in the eighteenth century. There were no roads. My Gaelic-speaking preliterate ancestors banded together in tribal groups—*clachans* or clans—in crofting townships. Their *bothies*—windowless, one-room huts of turf and stone—had dirt floors and smoke-holes cut into the heather-thatched roofs. They tore thin topsoil out of the stony moors and grew meagre crops of oats, barley and potatoes. But the drudgery of crofting life was relieved in the *gloam'in,* the half-light, when families gathered for *ceilidhs* around a peat fire. They sang the laments and pibrochs, listened to the *seannachie*— the hereditary clan bard—recount stories of our ancestors' heroic deeds. They kept our history and culture alive for centuries through the Gaelic oral tradition.

My Sutherland ancestors were proud of their status as warriors. When Samuel Johnson toured the Highlands in 1773 he observed, "Every man is a soldier." A clansman was trained to fight from boyhood, taught to belt out his clan motto as he rushed headlong into the fray. Murray lads, wielding basket-hilted broadswords and Lochaber axes, charged our age-old enemies—the Campbells, MacKays, Sinclairs or Drummonds—bellowing our war cry over the moors: *Firth, fortune and fill the fetters!*

The Murrays were renowned for their military strength, our history one of continuous clan feuds and wars against the British conquerors. In the legendary Battle of Bannockburn in 1314, the Murrays aided Robert the Bruce in becoming king of a united Scotland. On the bleak expanse of Culloden Moor in 1745, William Murray, Duke of Atholl, and his younger brother Lord George Murray supported Bonnie Prince Charlie's attempt to regain the English throne with three thousand Murray clansmen. Commander of the Prince's army, "Geordie" was celebrated for his inspiring leadership in the eighteenth-century Scots jig "Atholl Highlanders":

Wha will ride wi' gallant Murray, wha will ride for
    Geordie's sel'?
He's the flower o' Glenisla and the darlin' o' Dunkeld.
See the white rose on his bonnet, see his banner o'er
    the Tay.
His guid sword he now has drawn it and has flung the
    sheath away.

Every faithful Murray follows, first of heroes, best of men.
Every true and trusty Stuart blythely leaves his native glen.
Atholl lads are lads of honour, westland rogues are rebels a.'
When we come within their border we may gar the
    Campbells' claw.

As Jeff was heading off to Afghanistan, I sent him these lyrics along with a CD of the Battlefield Band's spirited rendition of the song. I wrote in my accompanying letter, *Dear Jefferson Clifford, All we Murrays ride with you every day. Firth, fortune....* I offered words as a talisman for my nephew. Since time immemorial, warriors have carried tokens or charms to safeguard them during their trials. "We've always turned to amulets," Jungian psychologist James Hillman explains in *A Terrible Love of War,* "invoking powers beyond [our] ken, recognizing war is out of our hands, that it is a religious phenomenon, mystical, mythical." I put my faith in the power of words, wanting Jeff to feel that the love of all his relations and the spirits of our ancestors would guide and shield him.

Sylvie called upon the religious symbolism of her Catholic upbringing. She gave Jeff a Saint Christopher medal to carry on his journey. In the third century, Christopher—a tall, robust man—voluntarily ferried people on his broad shoulders across a dangerous rushing river. One day, he was transporting a small child, who grew increasingly heavy. Christopher, battling the swift current, had never borne such a load. Gasping for air as they reached the other side, Christopher told the child that they almost didn't make it.

"You had on your shoulders the weight of the world," the child replied. "I am the Christ. I carry the burden of the world's sins on my shoulders." Thus Christopher—meaning "Christ-carrier"—became the patron saint of travellers. His statues and pictures mark the entrances to churches, bridges and houses. They often bear an inscription: *Whoever shall behold the image of St. Christopher shall not faint or fall on that day.*

Marion heeded the same urge to shield her son with amulets. She had read about the protective energies in gemstones. Desperate to try anything, she made her first visit to a metaphysical store, Little Mysteries, in downtown Halifax. She chose gemstones with renowned strengthening properties: a pinkish-grey-streaked agate for victory in battle; a shard of clear quartz for healing; a pure black jet stone to dispel fearful thoughts; green jasper to promote health and restful sleep; a black-gold tiger's eye to instill courage; a shimmering pink moonstone to prevent anxiety; and a black obsidian arrowhead, especially beneficial to Scorpios. She even followed the prescribed procedure to cleanse and energize the gems: exposed them to the rays of the sun and the beams of the moon above Eastern Passage, and dedicated their powers to safeguard her son who was now in a remote desert outpost. Jeff carried them with him on his final ride. The Saint Christopher medal and the gemstones, still within their shiny green drawstring pouch, were found tucked in a pocket of his uniform.

So too the Greek hero Achilles, the mightiest of warriors, could not be saved from his destiny. Even with a goddess for his mother, the sea goddess Thetis, a mother who dipped her infant son into the River Styx to make him immortal; a mother who disguised her warrior son as a girl so he would not be drafted into the Trojan War; a mother who even had a suit of divine armour forged to guard her son in battle. Still, Achilles could not escape his fate. He died young, slain by a god and by a man in the Trojan War. When Thetis dipped her baby son into the sacred river, the waters didn't flow over the heel she held him by. Many years later, the arrow of a vengeful Paris, guided by Apollo, found the unguarded spot.

In the same way, Jeff's talismans didn't necessarily fail: he did not lack courage, nor did he succumb to anxiety or ill health. He didn't engage in a battle, so victory wasn't an issue. On July 4 he rode in the third vehicle in the convoy— the first one without ECM equipment. Death found a loop-hole in his protections.

Murray clan stories, blue-green Murray tartan ties, scarves, kilts and afghans; clan pins and crests, inscribed with our French heraldic motto, Tout Pret—"Quite Ready"—pre-vailed in Jeff's upbringing and loomed large in his imagina-tion. During his late teenage years, he dreamed he stood on a rocky cliff, dressed in a kilt, holding a shield in one hand and a sword in the other. This same dream recurred many times. He was so mystified and troubled by the dream that he told his mother about it. "He was really disturbed that he kept having the same dream," Marion told me much later. "He felt it meant something, but he didn't know what." At this stage of his life, his adolescent rebellious phase, Jeff voiced intense opposition to the military. He had no inclination to become a soldier, or at least no conscious inclination. In the unconscious realm of dreams, however, was the guardian of his fate—his *daimon,* as Plato called it—reminding him of his soul's calling?

It wasn't until a couple of weeks after Jeff's death that I learned about these Highland warrior dreams. Our family had retreated to the cottage at Fanjoy's Point. Shell-shocked, consumed by our loss, we were just embarking on the long road of recovery.

You turn off southern New Brunswick Highway 105 onto a narrow dirt road. You wind past fields of strawberries into a tree-canopied funnel of time, past cottages built in the forties and fifties. At the end of the lane, you reach a light-house beacon and a red cottage set back in the trees. The rocky point exudes the spirits of wind, water, ancient rocks, old-growth pine, and its first inhabitants; their bones lie in an overgrown Loyalist burial plot a few feet outside the back door. This cottage has been the navel of our family life since my sisters bought it twenty-five years ago. It's a place alive with memories—birthday celebrations, horseshoe games; sun-filled days spent basking like lizards on the sandstone rocks between cooling dips in the lake; long summer evenings of wining and dining and saffron sunsets. The place we marked the changes in our growing children every summer.

As a teenager, Jeff labelled the cottage "Base Boring." He resented having to come here every summer vacation. But in his adult years, Fanjoy's Point became his refuge, a space to relax and unite with his extended family; it was the one place that remained constant throughout his transient military up-bringing, imbued with the feeling of home. He had his own separate room in the "bunkhouse" adjoining the garage. Its east window brings in the morning sun, the sound of waves lapping low on the rocks and poplars sifting in the breeze.

———

Two weeks after Jeff's death, I arrive at the cottage before
the rest of the family. I want to clean and air out his room,
make it feel less forlorn. I shove hard on the wooden door,
sticky after the winter's moisture. A closed-up, musty odour
permeates the air. And I'm enveloped in Jeff's familiar essence—his swimming trunks and T-shirts hanging from
hooks, childhood books and board games stacked on shelves.
A book of Foucault's essays, his well-worn Blue Jays baseball
cap, his sunglasses lie on the dresser where he left them,
waiting for him to come back, pick them up, take them down
to his favourite reading spot on the sun-warmed flatbed of
the rocks. I sink onto his bed, pummelled by his absence.

I flash back to my last time with Jeff, here at Fanjoy's
Point one hot July weekend the summer before he went to
Afghanistan. Our family didn't know then about his deployment, and didn't want to discuss the possibility—or prob-
ability. We buried our heads in the desert sand. Each of us
silently harboured our dread.

That July weekend of 2006, we are celebrating Marion's
birthday and showering Sylvie and Jeff with gifts for their
baby due in early November, the much anticipated first child
of the next generation. In the screened-in dining porch overlooking the lake, we feast on lobster—our family's madel-
eine. We suck the tender tidbits from the spindly legs, crack
the red tails and claws, dip the flesh into melted butter,
scrape the green tomalley and coral roe from the bodies—a
two-hour ritual of digging out and savouring every morsel,
while sipping copious glasses of chilled muscat from the Jost

Winery in Malagash. The lake and sky turn a fiery orange as Marion blows out her candles, and we gorge on rich chocolate mud cake, topped with raspberry gelato.

Then Jeff starts playing DJ. He has an uncanny ability to choose just the right songs to stir each one of his boomer-generation parents and aunts into dancing mode. He puts on the Stones' "Honky Tonk Woman." My oldest sister, Marilyn, jumps up, grabs Russ's hand, and they dance into the middle of the floor. Jiving together for as many years as Jeff can remember, they whirl and twirl, duck under each other's arms, in synch with every step.

Reared on a continuous soundtrack of Van ("He's my man!") Morrison, Jeff knows how to get his mother up. "G-L-O-R-I-A!" Marion struts onto the floor, her lips in a puckered pout, head bobbing backward and forward; one hand on her hip, the other pointing and wagging—a dead-on imitation of Mick Jagger. We bellow along, harking back to our teenage dances at the Oromocto boat club, stomping and sweating to Don Corey's band—"gotta shout about it. . . . Gloria!"

Then DJ Jeff plays the "golden voice" that will pull the youngest sister up onto the floor.

> Ah we're drinking and we're dancing
> and the band is really happening
> and the Johnny Walker wisdom running high . . .

I leap up to join the circle of dancers. As Cohen's monotonal voice sings about women tearing their blouses off and men dancing on the polka dots, I lift my orange tank top up over my head, throw it onto the floor, stripped down to my hot pink lululemon bra. Jeff doubles over in laughter; his face and shaven head glowing in the candlelight. Sylvie on one side of him and Mica on the other, they raise their Scotch glasses to the dancers . . . dancing into memory—*busted in the blinding lights of Closing Time, Closing Time, Closing Time.*

He leaves quietly at four the next morning to fly back to CFB Shilo. It will be three months later, in mid-November—after the birth of his son—that we will have our suspicions confirmed. He is in training for deployment to Afghanistan in February 2007.

So it is here at the cottage on Grand Lake, a couple of weeks after his death, that I have my dream about Jeff—the first one anyone in our family has had about him since he died. We have all been waiting and watching for a sign, desperate to feel his continued existence in some form. I awake mystified by the mysterious imagery, reluctant to talk about the dream when I first get up. But as Marion and I sit with our coffee in the early morning sunshine, watching two loons dive and re-emerge in the glassy lake, I describe it to her:

Jeff is standing on a high cliff. He wears a kilt, knee socks, a billowing white shirt. He waves his arms in the graceful fluid motions of some martial art, like t'ai chi. And he is smiling.

"It was such a peaceful image," I say. Marion looks at me, astounded, then recounts the similar Highland warrior dreams Jeff related as a teenager—the same age as his grandfathers when they enlisted in the Second World War; the age of St. Martin when he experienced the vision that changed the course of his life.

As Jeff was moving from childhood into adulthood, was he tapping into the buried self within? Freudians believe that dreams manifest our repressed desires. Jung interpreted them as symbolic representations of the dreamer's unconscious. Dreams during puberty until age twenty are especially significant, he said, particularly ones that show no relation to the dreamer's conscious situation. "Called 'great dreams' by the primitives," Jung writes in *Children's Dreams,* "they are like an oracle, 'somnia a deo missa'—*Dreams sent by God.*"

Jeff's dream connected him to his ancestral past and, at the same time, presaged his warrior destiny. It foretold ambitions that would take him another decade to consciously embrace. "The dream is an inexhaustible source of spiritual information about yourself," writes Joseph Campbell. "The dream is the private myth." And what of my dream? Without any prior knowledge of Jeff's Highland warrior dreams, I envisaged him within his "private myth"—the first sign that we were given.

After my grandmother died, my mother inherited my father's Second World War service certificate. It hung in her living room gallery of family photographs until her death. Then, at her bequest, the framed certificate and my father's military medals went to Jeff—linked by name, character and inevitable vocation to the grandfather he'd never known. My father died unexpectedly and unaccountably. When he returned in the winter of '68 from six months of United Nations peacekeeping duty in Cyprus, he couldn't carry the garbage cans to the end of our driveway without straining for breath and reddening in the face. Suddenly, my father— whom I'd never seen sick a day in his life—had to travel to Halifax to undergo medical tests at the Camp Hill Hospital.

A weekend in late April, we drove from Oromocto to his childhood home in Tatamagouche Mountain. He was staying there overnight, and his twin sister would drive him to Halifax the next day. Arms folded across his chest, he leaned against the veranda of the red shingled farmhouse— the house built by his father and grandfather, where he'd been born forty-five years earlier. He waved, unsmiling, and watched our car disappear down the lane. I had no idea that this would be the last time I'd see my father standing there, or anywhere. At seventeen, I still believed he was invincible, as rock solid and enduring as his name—a Cliff.

We visited him in the hospital two weeks later; an oxygen mask covered his mouth and nose, so he couldn't talk to us. But he spoke powerfully through his eyes, wide, fearful eyes that knew of his fate. We drove back from the hospital that day through city streets lined with leafing trees and lilac bushes flaunting their sweet fragrance. The car radio played Glen Campbell's hit song:

I wanna live
Till I get old

I wanna watch all of this grow

I wanna live, live and let live . . .

And all I could see was my father's face, his lambent hazel eyes. A few days later, a week before I was to graduate from high school, he died.

The medical diagnosis was pulmonary fibrosis, an environmentally induced form of lung cancer. The military's investigation concluded that it was caused by my father's work in a salt mine for a few years and exacerbated by his military service with the United Nations in hot desert climates—a year in the Sinai Desert in the early sixties, then six months in Cyprus. So this was the story we told ourselves, and others, for many years. But we now suspect a more disturbing reason for his sudden illness and death. Only a few kilometres from home, he breathed in the toxic chemicals that slowly and silently killed him.

In 2005 Canadian media reports disclosed the extensive spraying of herbicides and defoliants, Agent Orange and the more lethal Agent Purple, to clear brush for military exercises at CFB Gagetown during the sixties—the years my father worked every summer in the training area. Dioxins from these herbicides have been linked to many fatal health conditions, including respiratory cancers. In 2007 the federal government admitted culpability. Compensation payments of $20,000 were awarded to people who had worked at CFB Gagetown during the sixties and had since suffered an illness associated with these herbicides. These people, of course, had to still be alive to apply for the compensation—unlike my father, robbed of his life, betrayed by the country he had sworn an oath to serve.

After my father's death, my mother—a youthful thirty-eight years old—sank into a black pit of despair so deep that she couldn't get up in the morning. My older sisters were just setting out on careers as independent working women, and I was about to begin university. Her nest was completely and abruptly empty. With no other identity but wife and mother to sustain her, she lost her will to live. She was hospitalized for months, jolted with electroshock therapy, and sent home with many bottles of different-coloured pills.

When my mother, Marion Alma McGrath, came of age in 1940s rural Nova Scotia, men grew up to become farmers, salt miners or lobster fishermen, and women grew up to become their wives. Alma wanted to be a teacher. Until a summer Saturday evening in 1946 at the Malagash Union dance hall. Sweet-sixteen in her dirndl skirt, white bobby socks and saddle shoes, she fox-trotted with Clifford Murray. Twenty-four years old, he had just returned from the war overseas and was working at the Malagash salt mine. He had a prominent Kirk Douglas–like dimple in his chin and an irresistible grin. They courted for a year while Alma completed grade ten; then they married on a sunny afternoon in June at the United Church manse. She was just seventeen, a willowy raven-haired beauty in her brown wool-crepe suit, pink silk blouse, pink felt hat and a corsage of pink sweetheart roses.

Amid a shower of confetti at Malagash Station, they boarded the train to embark on their honeymoon. As it chugged out of the station, iron wheels click-clanging over steel rails, Alma watched the familiar landscape recede through the window, and the adolescent schoolgirl and obedient daughter slip away. She was Mrs. Clifford Murray, en route to becoming the mother of three baby girls, born within three years, her three Ms—each with "Clifford's trademark" dimple in her chin. When the salt mine closed in the mid-fifties, my father re-enlisted in the military. He served his country—often in faraway places—while my mother remained home, serving her family.

Our kitchen always smelled of something baking: bread, biscuits, gingersnaps, pies. The living room was fragrant with lemon oil burnishing the walnut tables and hardwood floor. Our clothes, sheets and towels smelled of fresh air and sunshine. Every Monday she washed them in her wringer washer and hung them out on the line to dry. On Tuesdays she ironed—everything (sheets, towels, dishcloths, underwear)—and starched and pressed all our dresses and blouses. Even in the evenings when she relaxed to watch TV, her hands kept busy, knitting sweaters, hats and mittens for us. She kept our home as spotless and orderly as the soldiers kept their barracks, ready for inspection every six months.

Those were "the tranquilized fifties," as Betty Friedan called them; women made careers of domestic perfection and lived lives of quiet desperation. Military wives, like my mother, endured the loneliness and alienation of living in PMQs (permanent married quarters) while their husbands were absent for extended periods on military exercises or overseas deployment. Just a few months into 1962, the year my father served in Egypt, my mother was so despondent that we went to live with relatives in Nova Scotia until he came home. When he was in Cyprus in the fall of 1967, I would come home from school at noon to find her still in bed. After that six-month tour of duty, he promised my mother he wouldn't ever go away again. In the spring of '68, just before his illness, they bought a small travel trailer, anticipating their dawning freedom now that their children were grown. But Clifford went away again—for good this time.

Two years later, the birth of Jefferson Clifford was a beam of light that lifted our family from the shadow of my father's death. He was like the magical child of the myths, the boy my mother had always longed for but never had—a saviour. *Every woman knows that the remedy for grief / is being needed,* writes Rita Dove in "Mother Love." My mother was certainly needed. Marion was working full time while Russ was completing his third year at university. And so began the extraordinary bonding of Jeff and his beloved Granny.

———

MARION AND RUSS bring their five-day-old son home from the hospital and carry him into the room that Marion has specially decorated for him. Red-and-white gingham curtains hang from the window. A red woollen rug covers the floor. A white dresser, draped with a red scarf, sits against one wall. A wooden rocker, with a red cushioned seat, waits by the window. They lay him in a white wicker bassinet with a red-and-white-chequered lining, pillow and quilt. A few months later, baby Jeff sleeps in a white crib with red flower decals. He lies on his back and kicks his legs, watching red teddy bears and white lambs circle around and around under a red-and-white umbrella-mobile.

I think about the strange synchronicity—the circle of red and white. They're not typical colours for a baby's room. But they would be the colours of the flag under which Jeff would one day serve—the Canadian flag that would blanket him as he lay in the white satin lining of his coffin.

II. CHILD OF DESTINY

———

In the myth, the child proves himself by confronting a physical force or by receiving a divine blessing. He kills the giant—the irrational authority of the adult who would suppress him. . . . Each of us has felt the frustration in childhood of being constantly thwarted by adults, of being treated as a child when we knew we were no longer one.

David Adams Leeming,
Mythology: The Voyage of the Hero

The child is the father of the man.

William Wordsworth, "My Heart Leaps Up"

ONE MORNING IN NOVEMBER, shortly after his fourth birthday, Jeff isn't at daycare as he usually is during the week. He's at home, trying to play quietly by himself while his dad studies for military exams. He watched his favourite TV shows—*Sesame Street* and *The Friendly Giant;* built tall towers with his Lego blocks, then crashed them down with the shiny silver airplane he got for his birthday. Now he's sitting up beside his dad at the kitchen table, covered with piles of papers and books—thick books without any pictures. He pulls a brown crayon out of his new Crayola box, draws a big cake—chocolate—like the one his Granny made for his birthday. Four candles on top—red, blue, yellow, green—and an orange flame on each one. He puts red hearts around the cake, thinking *I'll give this picture to Granny,* and wishing he could take it to her today. His dad doesn't have time to play; his head is buried in all those books and papers covered in lines of tiny black letters.

"Dad, can we go visit Granny?"

"No, not today," Russ says, glancing up from his book. "Mom took the car to work. It's a long walk to Granny's place, and it's really chilly outside. We can't walk that far in the cold."

"I can walk there, Dad. I'll put on my snowsuit and boots. I won't be cold. Please."

"Sorry, Jeff, we can't go today."

"But I drew a picture for Granny."

"You can give it to her on Sunday when we go there for supper." Russ gets up from the table. "I'm going to make lunch now; then you need to have your nap. We can play after you wake up."

After Russ reads Jeff his favourite picture book, *Little Red Riding Hood,* and tucks him into bed, he stretches out on the couch to read another military manual. He wakes up an hour or so later. The house seems unusually still. *He's sure having a good nap,* Russ thinks as he tiptoes upstairs and peeks into Jeff's room. His bunk bed is empty; only a blue-and-red comforter in a rumpled heap at the bottom. *He must be in the basement, shooting balls into his hockey net.* He opens the basement door; there are no comforting sounds of a stick scraping cement or a rubber ball careening off the walls, no reply to his calling—"Jeff?" *He's probably hiding, trying to fool his old man.* Russ hurries from room to room, peers under the beds, in the closets, behind the chairs. At the back door, the little black boots aren't on the boot tray; the red snowsuit is not hanging on the hook. He rushes outside; calls around the empty courtyard of their row house; races back into the house and grabs the phone.

When Marion answers, he blurts out, "Jeff's gone."

"What do you mean?"

"I put him down for his nap, then fell asleep on the couch. He was gone when I woke up. I've looked everywhere—in the house and outside."

"I'm leaving now—I'll be right home."

As soon as Russ hangs up, the phone rings.

Jeff strides along the grassy edge of Waasis Road—the town's main thoroughfare—with a Big Bird knapsack on his back. His red snowsuit gapes open, his boots flap unbuckled. His sandy brown hair blows in the biting wind. Cars and trucks swish past. A van pulls over to the side of the road just ahead of him. Two men get out.

"Where are you going, son?"

"To my granny's house."

"Would you like a ride?"

"Okay."

"Where does your granny live?"

"You go down this road. I can show you." Jeff watches out the window of the back seat as they drive past the soccer field, past the track where his mom goes running. "There it is!" he says, when he sees the red-brick apartment building on the corner of Gilmour Street, "That's Granny's house."

Alma has her hands submerged in a bowl of bread dough when the doorbell rings. *Wouldn't you know it—who could that be?* She scrapes the sticky dough from between her fingers as the ding-dong sounds again. She peeks through the tiny viewer in the door—two men in khaki uniforms, provosts, the military police. She fumbles with the safety latch and opens the door. Her gaze drops to a freckled face, hazel eyes looking up at her. "Jeffy!"

"Ma'am, is this your grandson?"

Jeff doesn't wait for an answer. "Hi, Granny." He breezes past her through the door. "I wanted to see you today."

———

As a boy, Jeff often revealed the courage and determination to "slay the giant," to challenge the authority of an adult who tried to block his intentions or, perhaps, his soul's yearnings. Longing to connect with his unknown grandfather-namesake, he would search through the stacks of old photo albums to find pictures of Clifford, and question his grandmother about each one. He'd sit in her rocking chair, staring up at his grandfather's Second World War service certificate, and ask if he could hold his grandfather's military medals with their colourful ribbons. He would rub his fingers over their shiny faces, wanting to know what each bronze disc signified.

One day, when he was in first grade, Jeff pleaded with his mother to let him take one particular picture of his grandfather to school. It was only a 2-by-2-inch, black-and-white photo, but it loomed large in the imagination of six-year-old Jeff: his uniformed grandfather sits, smiling, atop a huge Centurion tank. "Sorry, Jeff," his mother said, "but you can't take the picture to school. It might get lost or torn."

A few days later, Marion was doing the laundry and about to put Jeff's blue jeans into the washer. She felt something tucked inside the front pocket, reached in and pulled out his grandfather's photo—crumpled and creased from its journey to school and back.

Now, it seems that Jeff's grandfather was like a spirit guide for him—the semi-mythical ancestor who embodied Jeff's own calling. Thirty years later, when Jeff was perched in the commanding hatch of his LAV in Afghanistan, Marion taped this wrinkled picture of his grandfather onto her fridge. Beside it, she placed a photo of Jeff in his uniform, and the lyrics of "The Atholl Highlanders"—*All we Murrays ride with you every day.*

It's a Saturday afternoon in early November just before his eighth birthday. Jeff and his grandmother are playing a game of crazy eights at the kitchen table. He's staying for the weekend with her and his step-grandfather, Jack, at their home in rural New Maryland. "Granny, can we go to the mall? Jeff asks. "I want to show you this really cool race car set at Zellers." He flashes a gap-toothed grin. "My birthday is only six days away you know."

"That would be fun," she says, getting up to go into the living room. "Let's see if Jack will drive us there." Jack is lounging with his feet up in his brown velour La-Z-Boy, eyes glued to the TV—the Saturday afternoon football game.

"It's a tie game," he says. "I can't miss the last quarter."

Alma glares at him, hands on her hips. She has her licence, but hasn't driven a car for many years. As a young woman she learned to drive on rural dirt roads, but only got behind the wheel to drive a few miles to the shore in Malagash. She looks at Jeff's deflated face. *It's only six miles into Fredericton,* she thinks. *And there's not much traffic on this road.* "Well, then," she says, "I guess I'll just have to take the car myself. What do you think, Jeffy?"

"Yeah! You can do it, Granny," he says, eyes sparkling. "You're a good driver."

"Okay," she says, "let's go." They climb into Jack's new maroon and tan Oldsmobile sedan, two pals off on an adventure. She drives slowly down the long driveway onto the main road, her moist hands gripping the steering wheel. She isn't accustomed to the car's more modern features—power steering, power brakes, automatic locks, push-button windows. But the road is traffic free, and she's going well below the speed limit. There's just that one busy intersection with traffic lights where they have to turn left onto Prospect Street, she thinks, then the mall is right there on the corner.

Jeff is fingering all the shiny silver buttons on his door, curious to see what they're for and how they work. "Granny, I'm hot," he says. "Can I put my window down a bit?"

"Sure. Go ahead," she says, her eyes fixed on the road, hands white-knuckled in the ten o'clock–two o'clock position. Jeff presses all the buttons, but nothing happens. So she reaches over with her right hand, across the wide bench seat to help him. Her left hand jerks the steering wheel towards the side of the road. The car swerves. Tires crunch onto the gravel shoulder. The Olds careens down a steep six-foot embankment, and lands nose-down in the ditch.

Dear Granny,

I'm sorry about the accident. It was my fault.

You were only trying to help me.

Thank you for the delicious roast beef you made for supper.

I LOVE YOU

I LOVE YOU

I LOVE YOU

X O X O X O X O

X O X O X O X O

> *Jeff*

Twenty-two years later, we found the letter tucked away in her cedar chest. At the bottom of the blue-lined notepaper she'd written, *Nov. 5ᵗʰ 1978—Oldsmobile went in a deep ditch in New Maryland.* It's one of the stories engraved in our family's collective memory. It encapsulates their relationship—his grandmother's helper role and Jeff's appreciation of her unwavering assistance. This letter was the first of many that Jeff would write to his grandmother over the years, all of which she saved in the chest that kept her cherished possessions. These letters trace Jeff's growth throughout childhood, then his struggles with school during his stormy adolescence:

> *Dearest Granny,*
>
> *I haven't written you in a long time but you were a kid once you know how it is, lots to do, lots on your mind. I know I should write you all the time coz you're on my mind all the time, but as you can see I can't write to good. It's probably because I'm failing English cause it's really boring, but I'm going to need that credit at the end of the year. High school is alright, I like it.*

Jeff lost interest in school after the elementary years, and his boredom led to disruptive behaviour. At a parent-teacher interview, his high school English teacher confessed to Marion, "We just let him sit at the back of the room and read."

Mica is in grade two. She's marching with her class, two by two, down the school corridor. The only sound is the hollow echo of their shoes clicking on the cement tiles. They've been warned to keep their "lips zipped"until they reach the gym. Mica is in the middle of the pack, so she doesn't see him until she's almost abreast of him. Her jaw drops.

Outside the door of the seventh grade classroom, her brother sits alone at a desk, an unopened book in front of him. Her eyes bulge in disbelief, her lips twitch with the urge to speak to him. With a long questioning stare, she meets his eyes. He flashes her a grin.

Five years younger, Mica idolized her big brother. As a toddler, she wore his outgrown jeans, T-shirts and sweaters. She tried—unsuccessfully—to be included whenever his friends came over to play, yearning to be one of the guys. She worked hard at emulating her brother's proficiency in playing hockey, soccer and baseball. For her first day of preschool, Mica refused to put on the new white blouse, red plaid kilt and matching knee socks that her mother had bought specially for this occasion. She would not leave the house unless she could wear her blue jeans and T-shirt. When her mother came to pick her up at noon, the teacher called Marion aside. "I'm not sure how to put this," she whispered, "but . . . ?" She told Marion about introducing Mica to the group: "Today children, we have a new girl in our class. This is . . ."

But before she could finish, Mica interrupted: "I a boy."

From the outset, Jeff resented this "little princess," as he called her. She had usurped his throne as the only grandchild and the sole focus of his grandmother's affection. He bullied her constantly. He'd come downstairs to the TV room where she'd be curled up on the couch watching her favourite show, grab the remote and change the channel.

Mica would run upstairs to tell her mother; he'd call her a tattletale . . . and so the pattern perpetuated itself in many variations. While Jeff was slogging through the quagmire of adolescent angst, Mica was climbing high, achieving top grades in school and excelling in sports—just "a goody-goody," in Jeff's view. Once Mica became a teenager, herself, she no longer cared about his antagonizing tactics. When he came down to watch TV, she'd throw the remote at him. He gave up tormenting her.

In grade eleven, school took a back seat in Jeff's life. He was preoccupied with his friends and heavy metal music. Before going out on the weekends, he'd spend an hour in front of the mirror, styling his hair in a spiky upswept imitation of British punk rocker Billy Idol. Strumming his guitar, he fantasized about becoming a rock star. He developed leftist views and derided the military—its conservatism, hierarchy and itinerant lifestyle. He found his father's constant change in postings stressful—from Oromocto to Halifax, then to Ottawa, then to Winnipeg, then back to Ottawa— especially during his teenage years when he was severed from his pack of buddies with every move.

He skipped school, drank on the weekends and disregarded his curfew. Sometimes he didn't come home at all, and didn't call. He wanted to be in control of his own life and do things his own way. Russ had grown up with a strict military father, and as a soldier himself, he thought rules and orders should be unquestioningly obeyed. Power struggles ensued between father and son. They squared off in verbally abusive shouting matches that left a dense fog of tension in the air between them. Marion knew they needed a different approach to dealing with Jeff's rebelliousness, so she enrolled in a course—STEP/Teen: Systematic Training for Effective Parenting of Teens. She learned parenting strategies that encouraged teenagers to become responsible for themselves and the consequences of their actions. Late one night when Russ was away on a course, she had the opportunity to put the theory into practice.

It's after midnight when she's awakened by the ringing of the phone. "This is Officer Brant of the Winnipeg Police Department. Are you the parent of Jeff Francis?"

"Yes." She is jolted awake, all her parental alarm bells ringing.

"Your son is in our custody. We need you to come down to the station as soon as possible."

Jeff and three of his friends are driving home from a movie in downtown Winnipeg. Starving, they empty their pockets of all their change, but don't have enough to buy even a bag of chips. They stop at a 7-Eleven and stroll down the aisle to the coolers at the back of the store. Each of them takes a submarine sandwich and slips it under his jean jacket. They're heading out the door when the clerk yells, "Hey, you guys come back here!" Three of them take off.

Jeff stops and returns to the checkout. "We're just really hungry," he tells the clerk, "but I live only a few blocks away. I'll bring you the money tomorrow—I promise."

One of his buddies rushes back into the store: "Come on, Jeff, we gotta get outta here!" Meanwhile, the clerk is on the phone, calling the police. Jeff doesn't move. He hears the squeal of tires leaving the parking lot, and the pounding of his heart.

At the station, Marion informs the tall, moustached police officer about her plan to make her son seriously consider the consequences of his actions. He ushers her into a small windowless room, stale with recycled air. Under bright fluorescent lights, Jeff slumps at a table, pen in hand, staring at a blank sheet of paper. He peers up at his mother through the sandy wave of hair fringing his eyes; sheepishness and relief wash over his freckled face. "He has to write a report describing the incident," the officer says. "When he finishes, you can take him home. Or you could leave him here for the night."

Marion hesitates. "Well, Jeff," she says, "I think it would be good for you to find out what it's like to spend a night in jail." Struck dumb, Jeff gapes at her, eyes wide in disbelief.

"I'll leave you two to discuss it." The officer nods and closes the door.

Marion pulls up a chair beside her son. As they stare into each other's eyes, the cleft in his chin quivers. They talk about making bad decisions and having to face the adult consequences of them. Then she leaves him to complete the writing of his report.

Half an hour later, Marion walks out of the police station, her son gratefully by her side. In the car, they sit in silence for several seconds. "Mom," he turns to look at her, "would you really have left me there?"

"Next time," she says, "I will."

Marion still remembers the opening line of the incident report Jeff wrote that night: "I committed this dastardly deed."

Throughout grade twelve, Jeff attended school sporadically. He found its social arena—the cliques of jocks, preppies, nerds and metalheads; the malicious gossip and macho posturing—to be as cruel as anything the gladiators inflicted in the Roman Colisseum. He couldn't sit at a desk all day, listening to teachers prattle on about stuff he had no interest in. All that calculus crap; his fear of mathematics was visceral. And French, a total waste of time. When would he ever need that? May rolled around, time to study for his final exams; he couldn't handle the pressure. A month before he was to graduate, he dropped out of school.

The public school system was barren ground for him. In light of the intelligence that would blossom during his post-secondary studies, Jeff's conflict may have been a war between what psychologist James Hillman calls *tuition*—classroom study and learning—and *intuition*—primary wisdom and insight. *Cradles of Eminence,* a book about the childhoods of famously gifted individuals, reveals that 60 percent had serious problems at school. Thomas Mann, Gandhi, Albert Einstein, Winston Churchill, Picasso, Emile Zola: they wouldn't, or couldn't, learn in a regimented classroom. They hated school, and either quit or were expelled. "It is as if the image in the heart in so many cases is hampered by the program of tuition and its time bound regularity," Hillman concludes. "An exam tests more than your endurance, ability, and knowledge; it tests your calling."

There's a photo of Jeff—"June 1988" written on the back. He wears a navy suit, a crisp white shirt and a red tie. His chestnut hair is brushed conservatively back off his face. He clasps a black portfolio case under his arm as he's about to leave for his first day at a summer manpower training course—"Careers in Business." He's interested in becoming a stockbroker. Unsmiling, he looks off into the distance. Perhaps he's contemplating his future at the Toronto Stock Exchange? No, Marion tells me; he's saying, "Mom, hurry up and take the fucking picture."

Jeff's walk along the path to a potential business career is short-lived. In August, Russ is posted to Ottawa, and the family packs it all up, again, to move back east. Jeff is eighteen now, and a working man. He stacks shelves at Loblaws, busses tables at a restaurant and mows fairways at the Ottawa Golf Club. At night, he attends an adult high school, and completes grade twelve. Then he lands a job as a security guard at the Ottawa airport, working early morning shifts. In the afternoons, he takes courses at Carleton University—two in art history, one in biology.

In December 1992, just after turning twenty-two, he writes to his grandmother:

> *My job at the airport is OK. It's a dead end job, but I can handle it for now until I go to school and try to get a real job, and until I finish paying off my car I guess it will have to do. I haven't (until this year) been treating life seriously and I'm finding out now that I should've been a long time ago. I have to make*

73

*a lot of important decisions that I'm not sure about. Hopefully
everything will work out in the end. I'm sorry if you can't read
my writing, it's been a long time since I've written any letters. I
love you very much, Jeff*

In the fall of 1993, he starts the first year of a BA in mass
communication, immersing himself in the study of popular
culture and media, embarking on the intellectual quest that
will challenge him for the next seven years.

Jeff scans the sea of unfamiliar faces in the lecture hall—
the first class of his film studies course. His eyes light up.
Sitting near the back is Sylvie Secours, her smooth olive skin
and honey-blond corkscrew curls radiant, even in the dim
lighting. They work together at the airport, and both play
on the airport softball team. He's been watching her, mesmerized by her sunny congeniality as she checks passengers
through and chats with co-workers in English and French.
Captivated by her silvery blue eyes, he always freezes when
he gets close to her, grows tongue-tied, blushes as he throws
out some monosyllabic remark, wishing he'd paid attention
in French class. But drawn into her glow, he shuffles into the
middle of her row, and takes the vacant seat beside her. She
smiles, surprised to see him.

After the class, they stroll around the corner to
Starbucks—or "Five Bucks," as Jeff calls it. He marvels when
Sylvie tells him she's always lived in Ottawa, spent her
whole life in the same brick house a few streets from the
campus. "You're lucky to have roots somewhere," he says,

spooning the froth on his cappuccino. "My dad's been posted five times. I've lived on four military bases—and in twice as many houses. I don't know where my true home is."

In the classes that follow, they sit side by side, then pick up a coffee and chat about the films they're studying. One evening, after the final softball game of the season, they go out with the airport team for a beer. After a few rounds, their teammates gradually disperse. Sylvie and Jeff find themselves alone at the round wooden table strewn with empties, swirling the dregs in their glasses. They eye each other, and smile. "It's so cool how you switch back and forth between French and English," Jeff says. "I have trouble getting the words out in one language."

"You gain respect without having to say a word," Sylvie says. "I'm always nervously talking—worried about what people will think of me. But you don't try to impress people."

"Opposites attract," he grins, meeting her eyes, "a universal law."

She pauses, pensive. "I'm a floater. I skim along on the surface of life; get swept along by the currents. But you seem more like a diver. You search into the depths of things."

"But you have the sunlight," he says, touching her hand for the first time. "It can be dark and lonely in the depths of the sea."

He invites her over to his place on Halloween to carve pumpkins. It's their first date. When he answers the door in his orange polo shirt, they burst out laughing—she's standing there in an orange cashmere sweater. They reach their hands into the fleshy caves of the pumpkins, scrape and scoop their stringy, slimy entrails and slippery seeds. They carve one with a laughing face and one with a frown—like orange masks of comedy and tragedy. His mother insists on taking a picture, so he stands behind Sylvie, circles his arms around her. She rests her head against his chest and crosses her hands to clasp his forearms.

Long after the jack-o'-lanterns burn out, long after the smell of candle wax and charred pumpkin has drifted away, the two young lovers are still luminous.

In the back of the notebook for his film studies course, Jeff writes,

> *Silver is the way—*
> *your eyes are*
> *captivating me—*
> *capturing me*
> *I can't stop thinking about you*
> *And the way you make me feel*
> *DESIRE—I am so full—I feel I will burst into flames.*
> *I want to be the one*
> *to put my arms around you*
> *and keep you safe and warm.*
> *FOREVER & EVER.*

Sylvie becomes a flight attendant with Air Canada, and has to relocate to Halifax. As an Air Canada employee, she can fly to Ottawa cost free. By putting Jeff on her buddy pass, he also gets free flights to Halifax. Soon, he's visiting his whole family there. It's 1994, and posting time again— back to Nova Scotia. Marion, fed up with PMQs and the transient military life, resolves, *I will never move again from the province of my birth.* This time, she and Russ leave without their children and buy their first home, a two-storey heritage house on Williams Street across from the Halifax Commons. Back in Ottawa, Jeff moves into an apartment. Nineteen-year-old Mica lives a few streets over with a friend's family while she completes the math and science courses she needs to enter university.

A few hours after their parents have left for Halifax, Mica receives a call from her brother: "Are you doing anything tonight? Do you want to go to a movie?" In the next year, they become best friends. They go to the gym and work out side by side. They visit bookstores so Jeff can search for more titles by philosophers he's reading— Hegel, Nietzsche, Schopenhauer, Foucault—not for his university courses, but for his own personal study of phil- osophy. They chat late into the night about movies, direc- tors and books; have heated discussions about politics and religion. Mica grows frustrated with her brother; he's so logical and articulate in explaining what he reads, and his argument is always stronger than hers. She's amazed at his knowledge in so many areas—art history, Aboriginal spirituality, Buddhism, pop culture. It's as if he's shed his skin, left the sullen, cynical youth behind; matured into a thoughtful, erudite man. Already, she envisions him be- coming a professor.

Mica is accepted into the human kinetics program at St. Francis Xavier University, and follows the migration to the Maritimes in the fall of '94. For the first time, Jeff is living without the closeness of his family or Sylvie. He writes to his grandmother:

> *Everything here is OK. School takes most of my time. This year is tough! I'm just trying to balance—you know—like paying rent, working, school, car, bills, etc. It's good though—I like being independent. I feel better now that I'm responsible for myself! I really miss you. I think about you all the time. I love you Granny.*

On Friday the thirteenth of June 1997, Jeff isn't at Carleton's spring convocation to sashay across the stage in a black robe and tasselled mortarboard. It's not his style to bask in the limelight. But when he opens his transcript to see five A's in his final semester courses, he beams in the solitude of his room. Then he crosses the campus and climbs the stairs to the Arts office to pick up his white scroll—*Jefferson Clifford Francis, B.A. (Honours)*—his passport to the next tier of the tower.

———

As DUSK DESCENDS outside the classroom window, Joselyn Morley feels her attention fading with the light. In her notebook, she has a full page of doodles. It's the third week of Canadian Studies 5001: "Conceptualizing Canada," the core course for Carleton's master's program in Canadian studies. She wonders when, or if, it will get more stimulating. For three hours each week, the prof drones on about theories of knowledge, knowledge as technology, Ursula Franklin's warnings in *The Real World of Technology*. . . . The blank faces and glazed eyes of the thirty other students reveal a similar boredom or confusion. She can see by their fresh, unlined faces that most of them are several years younger, except for the guy who always sits in the back by himself—tall, shaven head, broad shoulders, muscular arms. He's older, too, and noticeably wiser. When the prof catches the class off guard with a question—a fitful attempt to involve them, or keep them from nodding off—he is usually the one to offer an answer.

During the break, Joselyn picks up a latte at the coffee bar in the foyer and notices him reading at a corner table, oblivious to the hubbub of conversations and Musak. "Mind if I join you?" she says, extending her hand. "I'm Joselyn."

"Sure. Have a seat." His face flushes. "Jeff Francis."

"How are you finding the course so far?"

"Well, to be honest, I think I might be missing something," he says, closing his book. "The theories she's hammering into us are pretty basic—knowledge, technology, language. All the stuff I did in my undergrad courses in mass comm."

"Yeah, and her tone puts me off." She grimaces. "The word *pedantic* comes to mind."

"No kidding. Not what I expected in a graduate course," he says, turning his coffee cup in small circles.

"I'm really looking forward to the course Pauline Rankin is teaching next term. 'Place and Space,' or something like that."

"Hey, I'm in that one too." His eyes spark with interest. "She's a great prof. I took one of her undergrad courses. I'm a TA for her this term."

Chairs scrape around them, and they follow the cue. Joselyn grabs her cup. "Let's hope the caffeine gets us through the next hour."

Throughout the term, they become friends, conversing during the twenty-minute breaks, and sharing their academic interests—Joselyn's in Canadian women's studies and Jeff's in Canadian culture and cultural policy. They joke about their common upbringing as military brats. "My dad was in the air force," Joselyn says with a wry smile, "and my mum declared herself a pacifist. So there were two camps in our house. In high school, my brother trained with the air cadets, and I demonstrated against American imperialism and cruise missiles with the Disarmament Club."

"I was somewhat of a pacifist during high school myself, or *idealist* might be a more accurate term," Jeff says with a knowing grin. "Easy to be a pacifist if no one's holding a gun in your face."

Joselyn rants about the frustrations of being a student and a mother—juggling kids, dogs, housework, classes, assignments—never feeling like she's doing a great job on either front. Jeff prefers to listen rather than talk. But when she questions him, he tells her about his family, and Sylvie, living in Nova Scotia—and how he misses them all.

Dear Mom,

I'm writing from my room in residence and from my window I have a good view of the trees that are turning color and there is still snow on the ground from the minor snowfall we had two nights ago. I am in the middle of reading <u>Away</u>, and I am also reading a lot of Canadian history and The Group of Seven and there is a chill in the air that at first notice is kind of depressing——but at the same time it is very comforting——as it gives a warm feeling inside me. I remember feeling this same kind of feeling last fall, and the fall before that. I never really understood it——or I never really tried to understand the feeling——even though some curiosity existed. It just felt really good. I think now I have realized what it means——why it gives a warm feeling deep inside me——beyond rational understanding. Autumn reminds me of that <u>place</u>——the innocent youthful place of love that I have memorized and saved since I was very young. Of coming home after school, and the sky was grey and cloudy, and darkness was taking over the day——and there was that cold breeze that would make your journey home a bit faster——because you knew that once you got HOME—— (that place) there would be warmth——not only physical but <u>emotional</u>——the smell of dinner, the excitement of family that somehow coincided with the season. Our home, though never rooted, was always stable——in the sense that love was always there. Sometimes never spoken or shown outright——but it was always there, and deep down——it was known it was there. The feeling that I get now at this time of year is recognition—— memories of the period when growing up and learning how to feel–and to experience the different seasons——Halloween,

Christmas, Birthdays, Valentines, Easter—will always be spe-
cial to me—because of those memories with my family and
especially because of your love—for if not for that—our ex-
periences would not have been the same—so thank you. I only
hope that I can pass that on, as you did, to my children one
day. Love ya mom, Jeff

The Rideau Canal is a variegated frieze of skaters and snow-
banks piled five feet high. Students hustle across the campus
in down jackets and toques, seeking refuge from the January
freeze in Carleton's heated classrooms. Inside Dunton Tower,
Jeff and Joselyn are two of six students seated in room 1212,
a small seminar room that smells of chalk dust. Book-filled
shelves line one wall; a bank of windows looks east onto the
canal. They sit on orange Formica chairs around a square
wooden table, two students on each side, the professor at
the front. No one spaces out or blends into the woodwork
in this class—"The Politics of Location." As fiery as her red
hair, Dr. Rankin meets their eyes as she speaks and challenges them with questions about the assigned readings: "So
after reading Rob Shields' article, what do you understand
about the concept of liminality? What are the characteristics
of the liminal state?"

Their eyes flit around the table, then drop to their notebooks. The steady tick-tick of the large-faced clock behind
Dr. Rankin's head magnifies the extended space of silence.
Jeff swallows, his mouth dry with apprehension . *The answer*
seems so obvious; it can't be that simple. He touches his upper
left arm where his tattoo of "the Void" is concealed under

his sweater. *The way of the warrior—facing your fear head on. Stepping into the boxing ring, bouncing at the bar on Saturday night, voicing an answer in this seemingly benign classroom— it's all a testing ground.* He hears Carlos Castaneda's Yaqui Shaman whisper: "A man goes to knowledge as he goes to War, wide-awake, with fear, with respect, and with absolute assurance."

"Well," he clears his throat, "it seems to me that liminality is a state of transition characterized by ambiguity. It's the places in-between, like borders and crossroads where people pass through but don't live. These are liminal zones. Or liminality occurs when people are in transition between one stage of life and another. Like after graduating and before getting a job, when your identity is unclear. As a postmodern concept, it seems to share the same semantic space as Bakhtin's notion of the carnivalesque." He throws out his condensed ball of thought. Its threads dangle tenuously in the air above the table, waiting to be pulled and probed.

Dr. Rankin pauses, a smile half forming on her ruddy face. "That pretty much encompasses the main concept . . . interesting comparison with Bakhtin. And so, Jeff," she asks, her blue eyes intense with curiosity, "how did you arrive at that analogy? Tell us about the steps that led to your conclusion." His face reddens, as he begins to explain, guiding them through the maze of his mind, gradually unravelling the ball of thread that leads to the centre of his thinking.

Jeff's university notebooks reveal an engaged student, a voracious note-taker. Every page is crammed with his writing—no white space, no margins, no skipped lines between topics or lectures, which are assiduously numbered. It's as if so many facts, thoughts and ideas had to be garnered and recorded that he might not have room for them all. The pages are teeming with the black or blue inked words of "the prof": passages from Claude Lévi-Strauss, Marx, Jung, Foucault, Joseph Campbell. . . . His small perpendicular script—a mixture of print and cursive letters—never touches the top or the bottom of the blue lines, but is suspended between them; the words float in space. In a black spiral-bound notebook for a sociology-anthropology course, he copied many passages from Campbell's *The Hero with a Thousand Faces* and *The Power of Myth*:

> The basic motif of the universal hero's journey is leaving one condition and finding the source of life to bring you to a richer more mature condition.

> If we engage in the Hero's journey, we will live life on our own terms.

> Trials and revelations are the means by which consciousness is transformed.

IT'S 1998, THE SECOND year of his master's program, and
the spectre of *the thesis* haunts the corridors of Jeff's mind.
He has always struggled with writing term papers. They are
not vehicles of further comprehension for him, but boring
exercises, drained of the joy of learning. So he usually post-
pones them until the last minute, then rattles something
off to get them in on time. But a lot is riding on this thesis.
He will use Foucault's theories to examine the CBC's role
in generating a distinctive Canadian nationalism. He lux-
uriates in the reading, the research, the thoughts that leap
and tumble around in his mind, the bright flashes of eureka
moments. He sits for hours with his adviser, Dr. Alan Hunt,
talking over piles of paper in Dr. Hunt's book-lined office,
or over mugs of beer at the campus pub.

As he contemplates Canadian identity, he ponders his
own personal identity—that shape-shifting entity he's never
been able to pin down. It's as if he, himself, occupies some
liminal zone—always passing through. He's not rooted in
a particular city or region—the Maritimes, the West, or
"Upper Canada," but connected to all the places he's inhabited, east to west. *I am a part of all that I have met.* First
and foremost, he realizes, he is a Canadian.

But he procrastinates about the writing; has yet to
tame his sprawling limbs of thought, and force them into
the straitjacket of ordered paragraphs and chapters. A week
before the deadline, he types all day and most of the night.
He leaves his cramped apartment only to work out at the
gym or to load up on triple-triples from Tim's. Just before
the office closes on the due date—April 30, 1999—he

hands over his one-hundred-page document to the secretary at the School of Canadian Studies: "Assembling the Nation's Culture?: The Relevance of Foucault for Studying the Role of the CBC in Emerging Canadian Nationalism, 1925-30." He does not beam with accomplishment, but sighs with relief: *Consummatum est.*

In late November, when the barren branches of Carleton's maples are stark against a steel-grey sky, he returns to the office to pick up his laminated certificate: *Jefferson Clifford Francis, M.A.* He shoves it into his backpack with his texts and notebooks, wonders if he will ever see it framed, on the wall of a windowless office at some university. Not an overriding ambition, he realizes. He thinks of his grandfather's Second World War service certificate hanging in his granny's living room, and his own scroll emblazoned with the chancellor's gold seal seems meagre, solipsistic. What do you do with an M.A. in Canadian studies? You go on to do a Ph.D., Dr. Hunt advised. So, wanting to resume his study of popular culture, he transferred to the Sociology Department and gained admission to the Ph.D. program. Those adult decisions about career path can be postponed for a few more years.

It's been five years now that he and Sylvie have been living in different parts of the country. They make the two-hour flight between Halifax and Ottawa whenever they can, spend long weekends and summer holidays at Fanjoy's Point, and manage to keep the flame burning—*tho' it were a thousand mile.* In the back of his notebook, he writes,

Today was incredible
—hours felt like weeks
God I miss you.
I hate explaining to people our situation
Why we are so far away from each other—they always give me that
    look—
you know—
that look that says—yeah right, long distance relationship . . .
—they never work.
I feel like saying to them
"You don't understand"—we are <u>really</u> in <u>love.</u>
You don't even know what that means!!"
If our relationship can last through that—nothing will come
    between us.
I think of you constantly . . . wondering what you are doing at that
    exact moment.
Sometimes I think I can feel you—your warmth, your laughter,
    your lips.
God, I love you.

Jeff strolls across the campus to the cafeteria and nods at a couple of students from his comparative literature seminar. *Sharks,* he thinks as he passes them, *out for blood—skewering other students in the seminar, boasting about their publications like so many notches on their mortarboards.* He knows he's lacking that cutthroat competitive drive—to appear "intellectual" with scholarly presentations and articles in obscure academic journals. *Thank god Joselyn is still here,* he muses, settling in with his coffee to wait for her at his usual table in the corner.

She bustles in, her long brown hair dishevelled by the wind; a leather satchel slung over one shoulder and a stack of books under her arm. "Sorry, I'm late," she says, setting a steaming cup on the table and collapsing into the chair. "There was a long line at the library. I had to get these books. A two-thousand-word paper due on Monday. I haven't even started the research."

"Having fun yet, Jos?" he chuckles.

"Fun? Who promised you fun?" She smiles, stirring her tea.

"Playing with ideas is great fun," he says. "If it starts to feel like I'm training for a bloody marathon instead of enjoy-ing the race, then I'll know it's time to quit."

"Maybe I should've applied to do my Ph.D. in sociology too." She frowns. "I'm discovering that historians stick their heads in the sand and ignore anything that smacks of innova-tive theory for as long as possible."

"Well, here at the higher echelons of the ivory tower," he says, rolling his eyes, "I'm finding an even greater gap between academia and the real world. A lot of the so-called knowledge that's being created seems irrelevant."

"Hard to reconcile sometimes." She nods. "And you just turned twenty-nine. I remember that milestone . . . the big three-O just around the corner. Questions about purpose and contribution starting to nag you."

He grins. "I thought the Ph.D. might give me a clearer sense of direction, but I still don't know what I want to be when I grow up," he says, chuckling. "No idea where I'll end up."

"Hey, a dissertation looms on the horizon," she laughs. "No problem with direction there."

"Another bloody marathon," he groans, sinking his face into his hands.

The white corner of an envelope peeks out of his mailbox. His grandmother's familiar handwriting instantly lifts the gloom he feels in the cool darkness of his basement apartment, her words like rays of sunshine:

> I hear you did great on your seminar presentation. You see, dear, you just don't have any confidence in your ability. You have proven your intelligence so many times. . . .
>
> Sometimes when I hear you talking, I wonder, how does he know all that? You are very well read and have a great memory. These are great assets. You are far too modest for your own good. I've got so much faith in you. . . .
>
> You are so precious to me words can't express it deeply enough. There's not a day that goes by that I don't think of you in Ottawa, alone. Remember dear you are never alone although it may seem like it.

As with every letter, a single sheet of notepaper——*I Love You* written on the outside——enfolds a cheque, a welcome supplement to the pittance he earns as a teaching assistant and as a bouncer on the weekends.

He sighs, weary with the weight of ten years of student loans and the perpetual emptiness of his pockets. In exchange for taking classes at the Ottawa Martial Arts Centre, he mops the floors and cleans the toilets. Living on $13,000 a year, he can't afford to buy the kind of gifts he'd like to give to Sylvie and his family. He picks up the book that he just bought to send to his grandmother for her seventieth birthday—*The Royals* by Kitty Kelley. He opens it to the title page and inscribes,

December 5th, 1999

> *Granny,*
> *You are second to none*
> *Your heart is full of courage*
> *Your "way"—nothing but grace*
> *You are the real Royal one.*

———

IT'S THE FOLLOWING June, 2000. Sunlight streams through the kitchen window as Alma kneads dough for one of the big batches of bread that she bakes every week. Her kids want to buy her a bread machine. They say it could turn out loaves so much more quickly and easily. But she needs to make her six loaves by hand. It's a ritual, an offering to her family. She thinks of them as she pushes and pulls the satiny mound on her wooden bread board, inhaling its yeasty fragrance. They'll soon be coming home for the summer, and she'll have lots of loaves in the freezer for them. Especially brown bread; Jeffy loves her brown bread.

The kneading is harder in the heat of summer. Her

forehead and hair grow damp with sweat. She pants with the exertion; her chest heaves. Gasping for breath, she collapses into her rocking chair. She knows she can't continue, or even wash the sticky dough off her hands before she picks up the phone to call her daughter. Marilyn arrives in fifteen minutes and drives her to the Emergency Room. An X-ray exposes a sizable tumour on her left lung. She stopped smoking seven years ago; quit her pack-a-day addiction cold turkey, hoping she might beat the odds.

"Are your legal affairs in order?" the grey-haired physician asks, scanning her medical chart. "You'll have to be admitted to the hospital immediately."

"But I can't right now," Alma protests. "I've just set my bread to rise."

Back in the kitchen of her quiet apartment, the daisy clock ticks. A mound of dough balloons on a floured breadboard for the last time.

———

JEFF SLOUCHES AT HIS DESK, staring at the blank white page on the computer screen. The black cursor pulses in and out, a mechanical heartbeat. He's waiting for the circuits to fuse between his sparking synapses and his fingers on the keyboard, willing words to appear. Finished his courses, he's now alone with his stack of books and computer, reading for his "Review of Literature" exam and attempting to write the proposal for his dissertation. He plans to explore the concept of *cool* in popular culture, to use Foucault's methodology to conduct "a genealogy" of cool—its evolution, its ethics, its geopolitics, its links to a political economy; cool as style, McLuhan's notion of cool . . . But the words won't take shape on the page. His head is too connected to his heart. All he can think about is his grandmother—the chemotherapy bombarding her cells, the chemicals shrinking her once robust body; her thick dark hair falling out in clumps into her white porcelain sink. When he talked with his mother last night, her fear filtered through the phone line.

He grabs a sheet of paper out of his printer and picks up his fountain pen. The blue ink flows onto the page, relieving the pent-up yearning in his heart.

Dear Mom and Dad,

I'm just taking a break from writing. Actually, I am having trouble writing—or with the discipline of writing. I am having trouble focusing and disciplining myself to write. I'm not exactly sure why—I know it's something very personal though—it has something to do with that deep inner self: I might have spent too much time avoiding it, and now that I have no choice but to face it—I hesitate, out of fear—fear of loneliness, or worse, fear of myself! I know that this is something I have to do, but it's not easy. Anyway, I sure miss you guys—I would do absolutely anything to be home right now!!!— enjoying sitting around the kitchen—talking and stuff. I have a thousand really good memories of being HOME—I really miss living close to you guys. I am really lucky to have a family like I do—you guys mean everything to me! I can't wait to get HOME! The days are starting to get really hot—humid—you

remember those Ottawa summers? It's going to be difficult writ-
ing. . . . Anyway, I just wanted to write you and tell you how
much I miss you guys. I am really looking forward to August
(maybe July) and getting back home! Take care—talk to you
soon. Love, Jeff

By the time the oak trees in the Halifax Commons are tinged rusty orange, Jeff is settled in the study his parents have fixed up for him in their basement. His books and papers piled high on the cherry-wood desk that bears the nicks and scars of his childhood. He's skimming through an e-mail from Alan Hunt, who is now his dissertation adviser. Jeff's pre-liminary proposal is interesting and viable, Dr. Hunt writes, but conducting a genealogy of cool could be difficult: "Like so many other tropes within popular culture, its popularity lies in the fact that it can be deployed in a host of different ways. . . . Indeed, what are the texts of cool?" Jeff needs to clarify his position, convert his document into something closer to a proposal, develop his ideas on the structure of the thesis; include suggestions about subjects for his two comprehensive exams. Jeff shakes his head at the jumble of words. He can't clarify, or convert or develop anything—he's leaving tomorrow for Fredericton where his grand-mother lies in an intensive care unit with pneumonia.

The third-floor room has grey walls and smells of disinfect-ant and medicine. A sunless north-facing window overlooks a parking lot. One side of her thin face against a pale green pillow, she sleeps; an IV pierces her arm, slowly dripping morphine into her veins. Jeff keeps vigil at her bedside, leans in periodically to listen for her breath; he finger-combs her sparse salt-and-pepper strands of hair, the vestige of two onslaughts of chemo. She wakes, looks around the room, bewildered. She sees him sitting there, and her brown eyes soften. "Jeffy," she sighs, "you're here. Watching over your granny."

He kisses her cheek, its familiar smooth softness. "I love you, Granny," he says. She smiles, as her eyelids droop. And she drifts back again, pulled by Morpheus into her fathomless inner world. He's there, as she slips silently through the thin veil, to a land from whence she returns no more. She never liked goodbyes.

On the last day of September, the Indian-summer sun warms the flat rocks at Fanjoy's Point where Jeff spends all day writing her eulogy. He feels her in the wind, a soothing presence hovering over the waves, lifting the weight lodged in his heart, so he can express in words what is inexpressible. How can the world go on without her in it? He thinks about the synchronicity of her dying on September 28 at exactly the same time as Pierre Trudeau. How fitting it is that she be accompanied *through the unknown, remembered gate* by this Canadian hero—a mother of three daughters and a father of three sons, each leaving a legacy of love and service in their diverse yet common ways.

As a state funeral courses over the nation's airwaves, Alma's loved ones gather in a small cemetery over-looking the white-capped waves of the Northumberland Strait. Jeff stands beside the black granite headstone of his grandfather-namesake, and eulogizes about the amazing powers of his grandmother:

> The world has suffered an incredible loss with the passing of our beautiful granny. Her impact was a blessing and a miracle in all our lives. She made us feel fully loved whenever we were in her presence, and the flame of that love continues to burn and give us strength. Granny always sacrificed her own comfort in order to calm and nurture us when we fell, or felt insecure about life's uncompromising processes.
>
> She could pull sunlight from thin air.

Jeff helps us dismantle his grandmother's apartment, a space exuding the warmth of a life devoted to her family—every wall and table covered with photos of her ever-changing children and grandchildren, a visual chronicle of her proudest achievement. The movers arrive to clear out her furniture and the taped-up cardboard boxes filled with her belongings. We're about to shut the door for the final time on the life that was hers when Jeff calls to us from the kitchen: "We forgot something." Wedged between the counter and the stove is her breadboard, still floured and caked with dough.

III. CROSSROADS

—

What is our true, our highest duty—to others,
the values of the tribe, the family, to oneself?
Is it to God, to a higher calling of some sort?
This is the critical question of the second half of life.
What am I called to serve?

James Hollis, *Creating a Life:*
Finding Your Individual Path

IT'S MID-OCTOBER, 2000. Jeff and Russ are driving a military van through the flaming autumn woods of New England. They're on a road trip to Virginia where Russ— Major Francis—will be working for two weeks, coordinating Canadian military personnel and vehicles for a NATO amphibious exercise off the east coast. In the sapphire skies above Interstate 95, Canada geese are honking their arrow south, so sure of their purpose and direction. During their long hours in the van—passing through Maine, New Hampshire, Massachusetts, Connecticut, New York—Jeff questions his father about the upcoming naval exercise as well as the elite forces in the Canadian infantry and the SAS (Special Air Service), an intelligence unit.

Although the Canadian Airborne Regiment was disbanded after the Somalia affair in 1993, Russ tells him, the Canadian military still maintains specialized companies in infantry regiments. "That's where all the exciting stuff is happening," he says, "where all the good courses are. The skills you learn are phenomenal." Early in his career, at thirty-one years old, Russ had tried to join the Airborne Regiment, lured by the adventure it offered. But he was denied—too old, they said.

"I guess you have to be super-fit, eh?"

"And super-committed," Russ says. "These guys will go on a thirty-kilometre day hike during their weekend. Not because they have to—just to stay fit."

"Cool," Jeff grins. "Sounds like it's more than a job—it's a calling." Long fascinated by the samurai class of warriors, Jeff wonders if the Canadian military's Special Operations Forces could inspire a similar kind of dedication and self-discipline.

He tells his father that he's been thinking about joining the military reserve as a part-time job while finishing up his Ph.D. "I'm really sick of not having any money," he says. "And I'd like to buy a car."

"That's a great idea," Russ says, smiling. "The pay is good. Once you're trained, you can work in the summer with the regular forces and earn almost the same salary. And the armoury is just across the Commons from Williams Street."

"I need a break from all the head work," Jeff says. "Maybe it would help me feel more motivated about the endless reading and writing. And make me more disciplined about it," he sighs. "I'm having a hard time staying focused."

He has brought along his books, so he can continue reading for his comprehensive exams while his dad works. At Virginia Beach, their second-floor hotel-apartment, elevated on stilts, overlooks the blue expanse of Chesapeake Bay. Every morning, he loads his books, some snacks and a water bottle into his backpack and heads down to the ocean. In the mellow October sun, he walks for miles along the wide beach. Then, stretched out on the sand, he reads—not Foucault and the other theorists he should be studying—but a novel his dad has passed on to him: Andy McNab's *Bravo Two Zero,* a true story of a British SAS patrol that McNab commanded during the 1991 Gulf War. He can't put it down. While the Atlantic roars in the background and the surf pounds on the shore, Jeff is behind enemy lines in Iraq, seeking and destroying Scud launchers, facing bitter cold, attacks, captures and torture.

The first weekend, they travel to the world's largest naval station in Norfolk, Virginia. They meet up with Jeff's second cousin, Matthew Francis, a sailor on one of the Canadian ships in the amphibious exercise. Matt takes them on a tour of aircraft and missile carriers, submarines and frigates. The base is in a flurry of preparations for a repatriation ceremony and the arrival of President Bill Clinton. Two days ago an American ship, refuelling in the Yemeni port of Aden, was rammed by a boat loaded with explosives. The suicide attack—courtesy of Osama bin Laden's terrorist group, Al-Qaeda—blew up the ship's galley and killed seventeen American sailors.

The following weekend, they visit historic Yorktown,

Virginia, where the Americans routed the British in the decisive battle of the War of Independence. Jeff thinks about the American soldiers who fought to the death on this ground two centuries ago—*they changed the course of world history.* On a brochure for the Virginia Civil War Trails Historic Sites, he jots down addresses and telephone numbers of recruiting stations for the US Army, Marine Corps, and Navy—unbeknownst to his father. Just in case. In a few weeks, he will be thirty years old. Would the Canadian military deem him, too, past his prime?

When they return in early November, Jeff withdraws into the cave of his basement study. Every day he sits in his grandmother's gold tweed La-Z-Boy rocker, cocooned in the multi-coloured woollen afghan she knit for him. A black-and-white-tuxedo kitten he's named Ammie, his Granny Alma's nickname, purrs on his lap. He strokes her silky fur, and thinks about Mica, continents and oceans away, teaching in South Korea. He glances over at his desk, at the teetering tower of books that he's ignored for weeks now; an envelope with Joselyn's handwriting nags at him. He received her letter weeks ago, describing her faltering progress with "that damned paper" and inquiring about his research and life in Halifax. But he doesn't know how to reply, how to articulate his state of ambiguity to her—or anybody. The rain pelts against the window, muffled footsteps and voices above, then the ringing of the phone. The door opens, and his mom calls down, "It's Sylvie on the phone."

He picks up the receiver, listens to her cheery voice enthuse about the party tonight. "You go ahead," he says. "I'm not really in the mood. And I should try to get some work done. I'll see you tomorrow. Have fun." The disorderly pile of papers—notes for his dissertation—and the blank computer screen glare at him accusingly. But they have no power to bring him back. Fogbound on a vast grey sea, he drifts without rudder or anchor. There is no safe refuge.

The steepled Wedgwood-blue building on the corner of Windsor and Compton looks more like a church than a Buddhist temple. But the sign above the door reads Ji Jing Chan Temple. Jeff steps across the threshold into an arch-windowed foyer fragrant with sandalwood. A low chanting echoes from the other side of the inner double doors. He turns the knob slowly. A spacious room with red damask walls, brass ornaments and soft candlelight envelops him in warmth and calm. He finds an empty cushion in the circle of people seated on the hardwood floor, their eyes lowered or closed. At the front, on a carved wooden altar, a large brass Buddha statue emanates tranquility. Below it, a man in a brown robe sits cross-legged, his upturned hands resting on his knees, his shaven head reflecting the glow of the overhead lamps.

The chanting ends, a space of silence. The monk opens his eyes and smiles. "Good evening and welcome. I am Bhante Kovida." He scans the circle, making eye contact with each person. "Tonight, and for the next four weeks, we will talk about what freedom really means, and if it is possible to be free in this complex society. We have a lot of knowledge—libraries full of books, many people with Ph.D.s or even

two Ph.D.s. We may be very learned and intellectually so-
phisticated, but unless we understand ourselves, our minds
will always be in conflict and we will never be free." A jolt
of energy vibrates up Jeff's spine as the sonorous accented
voice resonates in the room. "We will see that freedom
means understanding the self, understanding the nature of
thinking, and the nature of time. This is the journey of self-
knowledge." Jeff follows the flow of the monk's words for
the next hour and is swept up in their currents of thought.
He decides to travel with this guide.

He goes regularly to early morning meditation with
Bhante, and attends his classes in the evenings. He mounts
the cement steps flanked by lion-like statues, opens the
white double door, and enters another world—a place
removed from time and expectations, a sanctuary. In
this oasis of calm, he drinks in Bhante's words and feels
replenished:

> In truth, there is no self.
> Everything is a temporary mental state.
> Thinking is the root of all our neuroses.
> Impermanence is the nature of existence.
> We must die because we are born with a human body.
> Everyone dies but no one is dead.

He lingers after the class to ask questions, and Bhante invites
him into a small room off the main hall—a round wooden
table, four cushioned chairs, a counter with a sink, the smell
of tea and cinnamon. As Bhante fills the kettle, Jeff asks, "So

how does a Chinese-Jamaican boy, who grows up in Toronto, become a Buddhist monk?"

"In university, I had this crazy restless mind," Bhante laughs. "I was always worried about not achieving, about not having enough time. I had terrible anxiety about having to get a master's degree by the time I was twenty-five, then having to get a Ph.D. in biochemistry. I was caught in this trap of fear and thinking. I did not know how to get out. So I decided to try to quiet my mind by taking meditation classes at the Buddhist temple. And here I am . . . ten years later."

"Wow. That's a radical shift. It must have taken a lot of discipline."

"It was a matter of survival," Bhante says, lighting the beeswax candle in the centre of the table. "In retrospect, I was clearly on the wrong path. My head was full, but my soul was crying for nourishment."

Jeff breathes in slowly, inhaling the scent of honey. "University doesn't seem to satisfy me in the same way anymore. I don't know if the emptiness is because I just lost my grandmother . . . but I don't know where to go from here."

"You seem to be at a crossroad." Bhante gazes into his friend's sad eyes. "It is as if you have outgrown your familiar clothes. Your old ideals no longer fit. Perhaps it is time for shedding your skin."

Jeff nods. "I'm thirty years old. I have no money. I'm living with my parents. But I just sit around, not doing much about it."

"Sitting is good," Bhante chuckles. "I spend a lot of time just sitting. Think about the Buddha. He sat under the Bo Tree for seven weeks before the light came on. And Mohammed, he was forty when he sat alone in that cave in Mecca. Just sat, preparing for the quest of his life. Our society pushes us to be so busy—grasping, achieving, earning. But sometimes you have to withdraw into yourself, and just be still."

They talk late into the night, and many nights thereafter, sipping cups of spicy chai. The candle burns between them, illuminating their shaven heads. As Jeff strolls home through the quiet city streets, the darkness recedes—the first twittering of birds; a saffron sheen in the eastern sky.

———

IN 2001, THE SOLSTICE SUN shines down on a bus winding up the narrow road that leads to the top of Mount Tohamsan. A thousand years ago, Korean pilgrim monks in flowing robes hiked up this rugged mountain to Sokkuram Grotto, an eighth-century Buddhist cave temple in southeast Korea. They climbed in search of spiritual renewal, believed their arduous physical journey to the temple embodied the spiritual journey to Nirvana. Seated in comfortable plush seats, Jeff and Mica feel an inward ascension of travelling to a holy place as they curl up and around the serpentine road, spiralling thousands of feet into the striated mackerel sky.

Jeff has come to South Korea for a ten-day visit with his sister, his flight another perk from Sylvie's Air Canada buddy pass. Teaching English in the country since last fall, Mica visited the temple a few months ago, drawn by its renown as one of Asia's finest Buddhist shrines, a UNESCO world heritage site. When her brother told her he was coming to visit, she knew she had to bring him here; that he, too, would feel the power of this sacred spot.

The bus stops at a parking lot, a mesa on the mountain's eastern side. They step into the mid-morning sun, into alpine air steeped in pine and fir. A string of rice paper lanterns—red, blue, yellow and green—leads them up a path to a pagoda temple emerging from the side of the lushly forested mountain. They pass under an arched stone gateway into a rectangular chamber, its brown granite walls carved with images of ancient deities. They step slowly through a narrow stone passageway, run their hands over the smooth bas-relief sculptures, threshold guardians of the hallowed world they're about to enter.

In the centre of a rotunda, the Buddha sits cross-legged on a lotus pedestal. They stand transfixed, gazing at the five-metre-high granite statue. Under a dome ceiling, the Buddha's robust circular body, draped in carved folds of fabric, exudes an inner force. A circular relief of lotus flowers on the back wall creates a halo around his head, tightly curled hair, elongated ears, eyebrows shaped like crescent moons. One hand hangs over his knee, palm inward, fingers touching "the earth"; the other rests in his lap, palm up. A golden light illuminates the half-closed eyes, the faint smile on his face.

. . . the clouds of bewilderment clear away . . .

Have no fear: life and death are one in the void of nothingness.

Back outside, they rest on a stone bench in the sun, surveying the blue mountain ridges and the East Sea glistening on the horizon. "I've finally made a decision," Jeff says. "I'm going to join the army."

"What?" Mica turns sharply to look into his face. "You mean the reserve?"

"No," he says, meeting her eyes, "the regular force."

"Are you serious? What about your Ph.D.?"

"I'll finish it at some point. I can't focus on it right now," he says with long sighing breaths. "I need discipline."

"You'll certainly get that at boot camp," she says dryly. "Have you thought this through?"

"It's all I've been thinking about for the past six months. Ever since Dad and I took that road trip to Virginia last fall. Did Mom tell you about that trip?"

"Not much. Just that Dad had to visit some naval bases down there, and you went along for the ride."

"I'd been thinking about the reserve as a part-time job," he says. "Then I read this novel that Dad brought with him about British special forces. That's all I've wanted to read since we got back . . . war novels, military history, military strategy. I have no interest in the books I'm supposed to be reading. Then Dad and I went on a few wilderness camping trips around Nova Scotia with a winter survival group. I loved it! And realized it's the kind of physically challenging stuff I'd like to be doing all the time."

"Working out has always been your therapy, but . . . boot camp?" she says, grimacing. "Have you talked with Sylvie about this?"

"Yeah, she's encouraging me to go for it. She said, 'Whatever makes you happy, I'll be right there behind you.'"

"What about Mom and Dad?"

"I'll tell them when I get back," he says, rising and grabbing her hand to pull her up. "I wanted to be sure first. Now I am."

IV. THE VOID

To attain the Way of strategy as a warrior you must study fully other martial arts and not deviate even a little from the Way of the warrior. With your spirit settled, accumulate practice day by day, and hour by hour. Polish the twofold spirit heart and mind, and sharpen the twofold gaze perception and sight. When your spirit is not in the least clouded, when the clouds of bewilderment clear away, there is the true void.

Miyamoto Musashi, *A Book of Five Rings*

AT THE TIME, JEFF'S DECISION to join the military's regular forces seemed to come out of nowhere. We were blindsided by its suddenness, its radical deviation from his scholarly path. But with hindsight, the markers leading to his ultimate destination are clear. Growing up, Jeff thrived on physical challenges—on the hockey rink, the soccer pitch, the baseball diamond, the lacrosse field. I remember the sweltering summer of 1986 in CFB Winnipeg. We were in the backyard of Marion and Russ's PMQ where a three-metre-high wooden ramp was set up. Fifteen-year-old Jeff was practising jumps on his BMX bike. He sped up to the ramp, his sandy brown hair blowing back off his lean freckled face. The tires hit the front of the ramp; he crouched towards the handlebars, eyes steely with determination. He jerked the front wheel up and soared to the top of the ramp, flew up into space, spiralled at the peak of his jump; then landed, beaming with exhilaration. To our relieved applause, he smiled at us and pedalled back to go higher and farther next time. My three-year-old son, hands clasped behind his back, watched in wide-eyed wonder, mesmerized by his daring older cousin.

The summer of his eighteenth year, Jeff had to endure a month at "Base Boring." His father set up weight-training equipment for him in the garage beside the cottage. That July, Jeff developed his pecs, glutes and abs, as well as a lifelong commitment to health and fitness. His weight training progressed into a regime that went far beyond the physical. It was as much about having a disciplined mind as a strong body. During his decade at Carleton, he furthered this ideal—unifying body, mind and spirit—by practising martial arts: kick boxing, Brazilian jujitsu, grappling, and t'ai chi. In 1998, he enrolled at the Thai Boxing Academy and returned home for Christmas with two shiners. Since both he and his adviser, Alan Hunt, were committed weight trainers, they sometimes worked out together at the Carleton gym and talked about boxing. Forced to box as a schoolboy, Alan detested the sport. But Jeff told him that boxing gave him a venue for confronting fear, as did his job as a bouncer in Ottawa clubs and pubs.

Jeff's intellectual development corresponded with his physical and spiritual dedication to samurai philosophy. In 1997, he got a tattoo on the trapezoid muscle of his left arm that embodied this commitment: the Japanese character for "the void," the Buddhist ideal of emptiness of the mind. "Voidness is the eye of Buddhism," Miyamoto Musashi proclaims in *A Book of Five Rings,* a 1643 text on Japanese samurai culture. This mind—the way of the warrior—is essential in the path of the martial arts. "Warrior" is used in the Tibetan sense of *pawo,* "one who is brave." As Jeff underlined in his copy of *Shambhala: The Sacred Path of the Warrior,* "Warriorship does not refer to making war on others. Aggression is the source of our problems, not the solution."

A year after he was tattooed with the Void, Jeff shaved his head, another external sign of his internal transformation. In most spiritual traditions, head-shaving rituals mark rites of passage. For Buddhist and Christian monks, the "shedding" of hair is synonymous with the shedding of a previous stage of one's life, a bodily show of psychologically preparing for an ascetic struggle. Although the two endeavours seem antithetical—combat and spirituality—perhaps soldiering was "the way" for Jeff to further his search for the Void, a state of mind that can't be found by passively reading books. At age thirty, he was considered "old" by military recruitment standards, but he eschewed a desk job. He wanted the gruelling corporal tests of the infantry.

Shortly after he returned from South Korea, Jeff told his parents about his decision to enlist. Russ breathed a sigh of relief. He could see his son's waning enthusiasm for his doctoral studies, and that they were, in fact, depleting him. Russ felt that soldiering, which would challenge him both physically and mentally, would be a much better fit for Jeff than the sedentary life of a professor. Moreover, the military had been a fulfilling career for Russ; and in two years, at fifty-five, he would retire with a decent pension. Marion was bewildered by her son's turnabout, but she could also see that he was suffering. "He was too much in his head, kept too much within himself," she once told me. "The solitary reading and writing were too isolating for him. He was slipping into a black hole."

"The soul has a code," writes psychologist James Hollis. "The larger life is the soul's agenda, not that of our parents or our culture, or even of our conscious will. The agenda of the soul will not be denied though it may be repressed. It will show up in depression, listlessness, ennui, and fantasies." This Jungian view would interpret Jeff's depression as his psyche's displeasure with his life choices. Was he not living his own story, the myth that he himself had chosen? In "The Myth of Er," Plato writes,

> When all the souls had chosen their lives, they went before Lachesis. And she sent with each, as the guardian of his life and the fulfiller of his choice, the daimon that he had chosen, and this divinity led the soul first to Clotho, under her hand and her turning of the spindle to ratify the destiny of his lot and choice, and after contact with her, the daimon again led the soul to the spinning

of Atropos to make the web of its destiny irreversible,
and then without a backward look it passed beneath the
throne of Necessity.

Was "Necessity" intervening, disrupting the pattern of Jeff's
life?

When Marion told me about Jeff's enlistment, I felt
dismay and confusion. Abandoning his Ph.D.? He was so
intellectually gifted, and had climbed so far up that mountain—the summit was in sight. I also harboured many con-
flicted feelings about the military since my father's death in
1968—even though it wouldn't be until 2005 that we would
suspect military complicity in his illness. That year, 1968, also
heralded the peace movement. Ideologically, I lay with John
and Yoko in their 1969 bed-in for peace in Montreal, wanting to "Give Peace a Chance" and to "Imagine" a world where
there was *nothing to kill or die for.* I wondered if "The Universal
Soldier" really was to blame. As a pacifist, however, I had
never been able to resolve the problem of how to combat the
evil that exists in the world. What do you do when the barbar-
ians are at the gate? What would I do if the lives of my own
children were threatened? Speak softly and carry a big stick?

On Friday, September 7, 2001—the day of Jeff's swearing-in
ceremony—the Canadian military still felt like a safe place
to be, as it had been for Jeff's father and his grandfathers for
the past fifty years. When my dad was a soldier in the 1950s
and '60s, I never thought of him having a dangerous job. His
basement workshop, where he shone his boots and Royal

Canadian Dragoons pins, had a comforting smell of shoe polish and Brasso. Every morning when I came down to the small kitchen in our PMQ, my father would be standing at the stove in his uniform, stirring the porridge for breakfast. As the hymn "Holy, Holy, Holy" sounded on CFNB radio at 7:45, he'd put on his burnished black army boots, wrap the puttees and chains around their tops, don his khaki beret at just the right angle, and head out the back door to drive to the base. While he was in Egypt for a year with the UN peacekeeping force, I imagined him in his blue beret "standing on guard," as we sang in "O Canada" during our school assemblies. The pictures he sent back showed him bare-chested, riding a camel and wearing shorts—which he never wore at home.

When Russ served in the forces during the 1970s, '80s and '90s, the odds of a Canadian soldier being killed continued to be negligible. After getting his BA in history in 1972, Russ had a family to support, and the military offered a stable well-paying career as well as the possibility of adventure. So when Jeff swore his Oath of Allegiance in front of the Canadian flag on September 7, 2001, we weren't worried that he was committing to a high-risk occupation: Canadians were peacekeepers in the world. As an officer, Jeff would earn a significantly higher income than the average university-educated civilian worker ($73,000 versus $40,000 in 2002). But salary was not his prime motivator, nor is it for the average young Canadian interested in a military career, according to a 2005 DND report—*Military Ethos and Canadian Values in the 21ˢᵗ Century:* "Soldiers answer to a higher calling. They do not believe that money is the key to a good life. . . . They look for social value in their work, to be of help to others."

But four days after Jeff's swearing-in ceremony, everything *changed, changed utterly.*

Tuesday, September 11, 2001, was a golden autumn morning in Halifax. Marion had just arrived home, hot and sweating from her run around the Halifax Commons and up Citadel Hill. "Mom, come here!" Jeff called from the living room. "You have to see what they've done!" Mother and son sat together on the brown tweed sofa, the blue-green Murray tartan afghan stretched across its back, and watched two arrows fly into the heart of America: twin towers of concrete, glass and steel implode in an apocalyptic inferno. From the towers' tops, orange-yellow flames billow, jet-black smoke streams; begrimed bodies leap into space. Deathly screams, wailing sirens, blaring horns; ghostly ash-covered figures flee through the streets, the Manhattan skyline shrouded in a grey haze of dust and smoke.

It was the collapse of an old world order. Out of the ashes, a new Canadian military was born—a phoenix more in the guise of a hawk than a dove.

———

Saint-Jean-sur-Richelieu, on the west bank of Quebec's Richelieu River, abounds with apple orchards and cider houses, vineyards and wineries, maple trees and sugar shacks. But Jeff and the six thousand new recruits arriving here to begin their military careers will experience none of its pastoral charms. For the next three and a half months, they'll be confined in a grey monolithic structure—half a kilometre long and twelve storeys high—home to the Canadian Forces Leadership and Recruit School and the Canadian Forces Language School: "Apprendre à Servir" emblazoned on the coat of arms in the foyer. Not all of the eager recruits that are crossing the threshold will "learn to serve" and outlast the trials of the fourteen weeks. Only half of them will march in full dress uniform at the graduation parade in December.

With his disciplined fitness regime, Jeff is primed for the notorious ordeals of physical endurance—marching thirteen kilometres at 5 a.m., running six kilometres in combat gear, scaling four-metre walls and crawling through mud-soaked ditches. He glories in the field exercises that test his mettle: cold, wet, tired and hungry, he hones his samurai sword. And he's learned from his dad about riding out "the BS"—inspections for precisely folded socks and handkerchiefs, flawlessly pressed uniforms, cots so tightly tucked you can literally bounce a quarter off them. He resorts to the same survival strategies as his father did thirty years before. He hunkers down on the floor with a sleeping bag and air mattress to keep his sheets crisp, the corners taut, ready for inspection.

The arena he's not prepared for is the macho garrison of boot camp—working, eating and sleeping with the pack, 24/7, and the lack of privacy in the barracks. Several years older than most of his fellow recruits, he's an anomaly, a pensive aura still clinging to him. He dreads the predictable weekend prattle as the boys preen for a night on the town:

"Let's see if those French chicks are as hot as their reputation."

"Gotta pass that language course, eh. Best way to do it—immerse yourself!"

"Better tuck one of those French safes in your pocket."

His roommate asks him, "Hey, you're not coming out?"

Stretched out on top of his sleeping bag, his head buried in a book, Jeff glances up, tries to pull the corners of his mouth into a smile. "I'm beat after those drills. Can't keep up with you young guys."

"I'm sure you can find a bar that swings the other way, if that's your preference." Loud guffaws from the hallway ring in his reddening ears. And he suddenly understands—the smirks, the raised eyebrows, the whispers when he comes into the washroom. *Unreal.*

They troop out, and he settles into the serenity of solitude. He closes his *Canadian Forces Code of Conduct* manual, reaches into his backpack and retrieves Foucault's *Discipline and Punish: The Birth of the Prison.* He flips through the pages, busy with yellow highlighting and his barely decipherable handwriting—notes revealing the ghost of his former self. And he laughs as he realizes the irony. *Here I am in Foucault's Panopticon: partitioned space, constant inspection, a disciplined community, permanent visibility, a hierarchy of power....* But I can always retreat, he thinks, to that other tower—ivory, safe and secluded. When he read Joselyn's letter today, it all came back—that parallel world, that other hierarchy of power. He attempts to project himself into the role she describes—a sessional lecturer, trying to finish TDP (that damned paper!). But he feels a visceral chafing against his skin, the mould too rigid and confining. "I'm glad that you've finally gotten to where you want to be," she writes at the end of her letter. But he's not there yet—and still not sure how to get there. Lonely, he wanders through heavy clouds of confusion.

He's back in Halifax by mid-December, returned in time to help his dad pick out the Christmas tree. They always go to the same family-run lot on the corner of Windsor and North streets; he loves the sense of tradition, now that their family home has actually been in one city long enough to establish it. On a snowstormy evening, he's curled up by the fireplace, crystals hissing hard against the bay window, the lit-up tree glowing in the corner, the scent of balsam. The decorations twinkle with the geniality of old friends; and now his granny's ornaments have joined them—the angel shining at the top and the tarnished silver bells that were her mother's. He smiles to himself: *Granny in her Santa hat, rousing everyone on Christmas morning—ho, ho, ho! outside his bedroom door.*

Roasting chicken wafts in from the kitchen. The back door creaks open. "It sure is cold out there," Russ says, stomping his boots on the mat, brushing the snow off his uniform.

"You're just in time," Marion says, carrying in a bottle of wine, a platter of cheese and crackers. She uncorks a ruby Merlot and half fills their glasses. They swirl and sniff its raspberry and cherry aromas, then clink their goblets.

"Here's to you, Jeff," Russ says, with a broad grin. "Congratulations on your graduation. Well done."

"I can't hold a candle to you." Jeff smiles, alluding to his father finishing as the top candidate in his basic training. "You were amazing to do that well."

"But there were only twenty-two in my group," Russ says, "and a hundred and twenty in yours."

"We're proud of you, Jeff," Marion says, her eyes beaming into his. "And it was nice to see you graduate for once. Three times lucky?"

They laugh and sip, savouring the warmth. Jeff sets his glass down. "I don't think I can go back," he says, wringing his hands together. The fire spits and crackles, filling the heavy silence.

"What do you mean?" Russ says. "What happened?"

"I get totally depressed when I think about returning. It's like being in prison. *Partitioned space . . . continual surveillance . . . permanent visibility.*" He describes the homophobic remarks and the subsequent discomfiture he's endured. "And this time it will be for eight months. In a classroom mostly, trying to learn French—one more time." He'd hoped he was done with it after passing his language requirement for his M.A. Like a nemesis, it continues to plague him. And he realizes the irony, having been in a relationship with francophone Sylvie for the past eight years.

"Once you make it through this next phase," Russ says, "you'll be into your officers' training. It's a lot different. You begin to be treated like a normal human being."

"If you don't return," Marion asks, "would you resume your work on your Ph.D.?"

He looks down at his hands and shakes his head. "Can't go back, and can't go forward. I'm in limbo."

"That's a dark place to be," Marion says, "but you've been there before." She refills their glasses. "Maybe you should talk with Bhante."

"He's somewhere in India," Jeff sighs. "We haven't been in touch for a while." Bhante dropped by Williams Street one afternoon while Jeff was in Saint-Jean. When Marion told him about Jeff's enlistment, he was surprised, said he had no idea Jeff was contemplating the military. He left a Toronto phone number where Jeff could contact him. But it was too late—he'd already left the country.

"Think about how you'll feel if you drop out now," Russ says. "Becoming a soldier is not a cakewalk. There are times you'll want to give up. But you let that feeling pass. Then dig in again."

"I've got a couple of weeks yet," Jeff says, settling a pillow behind his head, "time to reread the books Bhante lent me, time to think about his words."

He descends into his basement study, enfolds himself in the woollen blanket his grandmother's fingers fashioned, stitch by stitch. Her needles click hypnotically in his head. He stares down the many-headed hydra of despair, fights the whirlpools threatening to pull him under. He sees Bhante pouring the tea, slowly, as in a ritual, the sheen of his head in the candlelight; the steaming scent of cinnamon and honey. He hears his voice, as warm and rich as his coffee-toned skin:

Unless we understand the nature of the void within us, we will always feel emptiness, disappointment, despair.

Freedom really means freedom from mental suffering. If the mind is clear and compassionate, whether you are in prison or have six months to live, you still feel peaceful because your mind is free.

It is easier not to take the journey . . . but then life can dry up.

He faces down his fears, and returns to Saint-Jean in January 2002 for French-language training. During the eight months, he develops a sustaining friendship with another "mature guy"—Scot Lang, married with two children. They swore into the military on the same day, and completed their basic training together, in different platoons, but sharing the milestones and the misery. Scott also studied sociology in university, so they have a common background of books. As they stand at attention during their graduation ceremony in August, the gravelly voice of a grey-moustached general resounds in the cavernous drill hall: "You never know when or where, but at 3 a.m. in some rain-soaked tent, someone will come through the door that you knew from your basic, and you will instantly remember the trials, and you'll feel that reminiscent and instant camaraderie. . . . There will be people whose career circle will constantly intersect with yours."

———

IN LATE AUGUST, just after Jeff has completed his language training, we're savouring the last summer weekend at Fanjoy's Point. We buy a cornucopia of vegetables from Slocum's Farm, just down the road, and cook a harvest dinner—cobs of sweet Peaches-and-Cream corn, a hodge-podge of steamed green beans, peas, carrots and potatoes, slathered in butter and cream. The long dining table in the porch shines with Alma's gilt-edged china and wedding silverware. After dinner, we linger in the candlelight, sipping oaky Chardonnay as the sun burns orange into the lake, and the crickets call—*summer's gone, summer's gone.*

From the kitchen, the clatter of pots, swooshing of water, trills of laughter as Jeff and Sylvie clean up the dishes. Van Morrison croons in the background. I turn in my chair, about to go to the fridge for some wine, but sit back down, not wanting to disrupt the tableau in the kitchen. Her honey-brown curls waterfalling against his shoulder, Jeff and Sylvie dance in a close embrace:

> Out on the highways and the by-ways all alone
> I'm still searching for, searching for my home . . .
> It's a hard road even my best friends they don't know
> And I'm searching for, searching for the philosopher's
>   stone

It was their last waltz—or embrace—for many, many months. Van's lyrics were like an oracular summation of Jeff's restless spirit, and the detour it would take him on over the next two years.

That fall, he severed communication with Sylvie. He didn't answer her calls or e-mails. "It's over for now," is the only response he gave to his parents' questions. And all that Sylvie could fathom is that they "weren't on the same page." Now that Jeff's career was underway, she had a vision of them living together—finally, after ten years of long distance. In her early thirties, she heard her biological clock ticking, loudly, and wanted to start a family. But Jeff didn't share her domestic dream. He was still polishing his sword, trying to see himself clearly in its sheen. Unable to handle the pressure of her expectations, he withdrew.

Sylvie left Halifax, and moved to Toronto. She put a down payment on a condo under development on King Street West, a trendy new area of coffee shops and restaurants near the lakeshore. She had a busy cosmopolitan life—flying around the world with Air Canada, attending film festivals, holidaying in the tropics with her girlfriends. But she never gave up hope that she and Jeff would reunite; nor did Marion and Russ, with whom she still kept in touch by phone and e-mail. Sylvie intuited that something wasn't finished between them. Even though her friends told her she was crazy, she waited, weaving and reweaving her tapestry's vision. She warded off the suitors and waited for her Odysseus to find his way home.

The Hero's journey is a lonely one, Joseph Campbell writes. *Privation and suffering alone open the mind to all that is hidden to others.*

THE FALL OF 2002, Jeff comes full circle, back to the New Brunswick town nestled between the two rivers where he was born thirty-two years earlier. At CFB Gagetown's Combat Training Centre, he marches on the same parade squares, traverses the same open fields; tromps through the same jungle-like woods and swamps, hikes up the same hills as his father and his grandfathers before him. The British officer instructing in the infantry school is harsh and demeaning, so Jeff—along with eight of the eleven other soldiers in the course—transfer into the artillery school.

Phase three of officers' training is technical: artillery instruction, involving trigonometry, angles, graphs. . . . So he finally has to confront his fear of mathematics. "You're a bit resistant at times," says his instructor, Captain Shawn Fortin, "because you're too smart for your own good and can see through the crap." Jeff fails the course, and has to weigh his options. Go back into infantry? Quit? He heeds his father's advice and repeats the course. He buckles down, studies hard and passes. Phase four, the final stage, focuses on the dynamics of leadership. He excels, and at graduation he's awarded a silver watch for top candidate—Lieutenant Jeff Francis.

His first posting in September 2004 brings him back to the big skies of southern Manitoba, to the sand dunes and rolling hills of CFB Shilo. He joins the First Regiment of the Royal Canadian Horse Artillery, the oldest unit of the Canadian Forces. On a crisp fall morning, hoarfrost whitening the lawns in front of headquarters, he enters a theatre-style room, a smaller version of a lecture hall at

Carleton—blue upholstered seats in rising tiers, a podium and a whiteboard at the front. The chattering and chuckling subside as thirty soldiers in green relish-pattern uniforms straighten in their chairs. Jeff nods. His sweaty hands open his black hardcover notebook to the list of tasks and reminders; written in military acronyms and shorthand, they're now an indecipherable blur. Sixty eyes size him up—their new leader, fresh out of officers' school—green horns to match his uniform. Many are seasoned soldiers—like the tall blond sergeant smiling in the front row, a senior NCO with seventeen years' experience and deployments to Cyprus and Bosnia.

He clears his throat, and wishes to god he could control the blood rushing to his face: "I'm Lieutenant Francis. I've just arrived from Gagetown where I've been training for the past two years. I studied sociology at Carleton University before enlisting. I'm originally from . . . everywhere, man . . . Oromocto, Halifax, Winnipeg, Ottawa . . . ," he says in a mock singing voice. A few grins and twitters of laughter loosen the tension in the air. "I'm brand new to the regiment, so I'll be relying on the sergeant major and master bombardier for guidance and advice." He acknowledges two soldiers seated side by side in the front row. "My intent today is to give you an overview of where C Battery will be headed in the next year. I'll keep it brief and try not to bore you to death.

"The next year is filled with uncertainty. But we know that Operation Athena, the Afghanistan Mission, is our main priority up to January 2005. The army wants two brigade groups ready to deploy sometime in 2006. C Battery will probably get another FOO party, and we'll have to be ready to provide fire support to 2 Princess Patricia's Canadian Light Infantry and brigade operations.

"On a more personal note," he says, meeting their eyes as he scans the rows, "I have to stress the importance of not getting in shit on the weekends." Feet shuffle, glances and smirks dart sideways. "Whenever you are drinking, remember you are not a civilian. They can get away with fucking up. We can't! We will be held accountable for what we do outside of work. I don't want to see any of your careers affected by something stupid like 'misuse of alcohol.' We are professional soldiers, proud of who we are and what we do.

"Now I'd like to open up the floor to you, and answer any questions." He closes his notebook and folds his hands on the podium.

"Sir, what are we in for as far as physical training goes?" a voice from the back row calls out in a lilting Newfie accent. "Rumour has it that you've been seen at the gym every day since you arrived." Laughter peals around the room.

"Let's just say, you'll get fit, if you're not already." Jeff grins. "I subscribe to the 'train hard, fight early' philosophy. Let's face it; that's what we're here for. And I truly believe in the ancient Chinese proverb *The more we sweat in training, the less we bleed in battle.*"

After the last soldier has left the room, he turns out the lights and exhales in relief. He steps into the corridor and halts, clicks his heels together. "Sir," he says with a brisk salute. The C Battery captain looks over his shoulder as if to check for a senior officer behind him.

"It's okay, Jeff," the dark-haired man says, and smiles. "Relax. I'm not 'sir,' or 'Captain Etherlston' but 'Craig.'"

"Yes sir," Jeff blushes. "I mean Craig, sir." And they both erupt into laughter.

"How about joining us for happy hour tonight?" Craig asks. "A bunch of us are driving into Brandon around five, meeting at the usual watering hole."

"Thanks," Jeff says. "I have a match at six—at the Brandon Boxing Club. So I'll catch up with you later."

"Such dedication," Craig shakes his head, " . . . even on a Friday night!"

Accumulate practice day by day, and hour by hour. Polish the twofold spirit heart and mind, and sharpen the twofold gaze perception and sight.

On November 11, 2004, Jeff is falling thousands of metres through the herringbone sky above Trenton, Ontario—developing his wings. He requested the posting to C Battery, the "Light Battery" that performs airborne operations, so he could take the military parachutist course and earn his parachute wings. He's in the hangar of the Canadian Forces Advanced Land Warfare School, still in his parachute harness, when the instructor enters to tell him there's a phone call.

"'Happy birthday to you,'" his parents sing over the line. "How does it feel to be thirty-four?"

"Awesome!" He describes tumbling head over heels out of the back of an airplane. "Remember that feeling, Dad?"

His father also took the parachutist course, decades ago. "What a rush!" They can practically hear the big grin lighting up his face, and remember him soaring through the air on his BMX. He doesn't tell them about his hard landing last week—the bloody gash to his head, the ambulance ride to the hospital—only about the weightless thrill of free-falling through pillows of clouds.

It's a crystal-clear starry night in Eastern Passage, the day after Christmas 2004. Jeff is helping his parents load up the dishwasher when the phone rings. "Hi, Sylvie," Marion says, glancing over at Jeff. "Good to hear from you. How's the weather in Toronto? Oh—you're in Halifax overnight on a layover?"

Jeff takes the receiver and they talk for a few minutes. Then he gets into his parents' Mazda van and makes the half-hour trip across the harbour to pick up the woman he forsook, but could never forget. She's standing alone under the indigo canopy of the Lord Nelson, shivering in the cold light of the entrance, her chin tucked into the collar of her black coat. Her eyes brighten as he pulls up to the curb. "*Secours,*" he whispers into her hair, wrapping her in his arms.

"Hey baby," she sighs. "It's been a long time." Two years. It seems like twenty.

"It had nothing to do with you," he tells her, as they drive across the lighted arch of the Murray Mackay Bridge. "I couldn't see where I was going. I missed you—thought I'd probably lost you forever."

"'Hope is the thing with feathers,'" she quotes, clasping his hand. "It fluttered, flew away some stormy nights; but was always perched there again, singing, in the morning."

They sit on the rose-flowered sofa in the dim light, only the glow of the Christmas tree and a white pillar candle on the coffee table. Through the black picture window, twinkling galaxies pulse down over the ocean. The incoming tide swashes the shore. "How's the life of a soldier?" she asks, warming her hands around a mug of hot chocolate.

"I guess it doesn't really feel like a job. I love what I'm doing; learning, teaching, feeling challenged. It's my job to stay fit!" he chuckles. "Next month, I'll get my captain's stripe. And start training for the Army Mountain Man Competition." He turns to face her, rests his arm on the back of the sofa behind her head. "The fog has lifted; the way seems so much clearer. And I'd like you to be there with me," he says, stroking her hair. "I'm ready now for the white picket fence . . . and the pattering of little feet. Would you move to Shilo?"

"Whoa," she says, setting her cup on the table. "I just bought a condo. It won't be finished for another year. I'm enjoying my job too. . . . independence. We'll have to see how it goes . . . *que sera, sera*."

"C'est vrai," he grins and gazes out into the darkness. "It's all written in those stars winking up there. Right now, it's like they're all laughing."

They talk through the night, as the stars fade out and a ridge of red rises over the eastern sea.

———

February 2005. Chief of Defence Staff Rick Hillier submits his defence policy: overhaul the Canadian military; deploy Canadian troops into southern Afghanistan; bring them home by early 2007.

Prime Minister Paul Martin objects to the cost.

The military will find a way to carry out the mission within its budget, the general assures him.

No one utters the word war.

The fat wet snowflakes falling in Edmonton on August 31, 2005, the day of the annual Army Mountain Man Competition, only reinforce the mood of the toughest physical challenge in the military. At the starting line, Jeff is lined up with 340 competitors shouldering sixteen-kilogram backpacks. At the crack of the gun, he takes off with the pack, jockeying for space and finding his pace for this first stage of the marathon—a run of thirty kilometres. He hits his stride, and feels he could run forever. He reaches a checkpoint piled up with fifteen-kilogram sandbags, and tucks one under each arm to begin the second leg of the marathon—the simulation of a canoe portage. He runs for three kilometres carrying almost fifty kilos, suffering the strain and the pain with every footfall. At the North Saskatchewan River, he trades his sandbags for an aluminum canoe and paddles solo for ten kilometres, battling the icy wind all the way. He lands his canoe, straps on his heavy rucksack again and runs again for the final six kilometres—his purple T-shirt and navy shorts damp against his skin, his face wrought with exhaustion and grim determination; his eyes focused ahead on a distant goal: *to strive, to seek, to find, and not to yield.*

As he crosses the finish line, the red digits on the clock flash before him—5 hrs: 32 min. Thirty-two competitors clocked in before him—but more than three hundred are still panting their way to the end.

Autumn 2005: Two thousand Canadian soldiers arrive in southern Afghanistan for a one-year assignment.

By January 2006, after the physical trial of the Army Mountain Man, Jeff is ready to transfer to an area of soldiering that's less taxing on his thirty-five-year-old body. The field of military intelligence has always intrigued him, but it's notoriously difficult to penetrate. The Intelligence Branch comprises only 1 percent of the total regular forces. Nonetheless, he applies and secures an interview. Within weeks, he is accepted into the Canadian Forces School of Military Intelligence in Kingston, Ontario. His C Battery commander, however, is less than thrilled by the news: "Captain Francis, I'll be frank. We don't want to lose you. You're a mature, reliable officer, highly respected by the soldiers in the regiment. Before moving into intelligence, you are well advised to get some real ground-level combat experience—in Afghanistan."

The regiment has an opening for another FOO (forward observation officer, pronounced *Fooh* in conversation), the most sought-after position in the artillery, the major explains; and Hillier's reorganization of the forces has created a special operations command. "Having a tour as a FOO in Afghanistan would make you a strong candidate for special operations," he says. "Few soldiers are accepted into this course, but I will recommend you for FOO training."

Jeff knows the course would be demanding, with a focus on mathematics and trigonometry, but he's already tackled that bogey. Another, deeper fear surfaces. As forward observation officer, he would have one of the most dangerous jobs in the army. The FOO operates at the front end of the front lines, scrutinizing the enemy's position, coordinating and calling in artillery support—guns, mortars and attack helicopters. He imagines Nich's broad smiling face, his comrade at CFB Shilo—Captain Nichola Goddard—perched in the commander's hatch of her LAV in Afghanistan, exposed to the enemy, the first FOO to call artillery fire on enemy targets since the Korean War.

"The longer we are in the theatre and the more we actually interact with the Afghan people," she wrote, "the more I feel we are serving a purpose here. They are trying to achieve something that we in Canada have long since taken for granted. . . . We are here to assist that legitimate and democratically elected government."

Deployment to Afghanistan flashes like a beacon on a distant shore: the opportunity to make a difference to a country in chaos, to help a people denied basic human rights of freedom and safety, and to combat a tyrannical force threatening the security of his own county. The bespectacled face of the Dalai Lama shines before him as the monk's voice echoes through his mind—*Today's world, whole world almost one body. One thing happens in some distant place, the repercussions reach your own place.*

On February 14, he procures leave from his FOO course in CFB Gagetown to fly to Toronto and surprise Sylvie with a Valentine's visit in her new condo. They relax on her white overstuffed sofa, smelling the yellow roses on the coffee table, watching bubbles rise in their flutes of Veuve Clicquot. Sylvie raises her glass. "Here's to no more birth control," she says, with a wide pearly smile. "*Que sera, sera.*"

"Seems like the perfect day to test the waters," he laughs and squeezes her hand.

His smile fades as he sets down his glass. "I don't know if it's the right time to tell you this, but . . . it's just been confirmed. I'll be going to Afghanistan a year from now, February 2007."

His words hang heavy in the small space of air between them.

"I know you really believe in this," she says, eyes welling up with tears. In their many discussions about Afghanistan, he's reiterated that the mission is more than a simple play for power, that the West can't turn its back on the country as it did with Rwanda. She knows it's something he has to do, something bigger than himself. "I just want you to go and get it over with."

"I need to do just this one tour," he says, putting his arm around her. "Then I'll try to transfer to an administrative position at the Downsview Base here in Toronto. Maybe we'll buy a house if we need more room . . ."

"We won't be together again until Easter," she says, snuggling against him, "so we'd better make *carpe diem* our motto."

On the twenty-ninth of March, he gets in from the training area to find a message tacked to his door: *Call Sylvie—ASAP.* When she answers the phone, he blurts out, "Is anything wrong?"

"Everything is so right," she giggles. "Are you sitting down . . . *Dad?*"

"Are you serious? Already?"

"Yeah," she says, laughing, "Cupid's aim was dead-on!"

On Easter weekend in Eastern Passage, the Russian willow trees bud lime green, and crocuses nudge their noses through the gardens along Shore Road. The salty air is sweet with spring. Jeff and Sylvie arrive from the airport with Russ, welcomed home by the aroma of baking ham and roasting potatoes, and Marion's warm hugs. "You must be starving," she says. "Was the flight delayed?"

"We had to make a stop at Chapters," Russ says. "Jeff had to run in to pick up a book."

They gather around the wooden dining table, an Easter lily blooming its heady perfume. Marion lifts a bottle of Jost Pinot Grigio from the wine cooler, and is about to pour a glass for Sylvie. "None for me, thanks," she says, placing her hand over the rim and kicking Jeff under the table.

"You're not feeling well?" Marion asks, looking puzzled.

"Ah . . . we've got some news," Jeff blushes. He pulls a

book out of a shopping bag and lays it on the red brocade tablecloth.

Marion and Russ squint, scan the title—*Fatherhood for Dummies*—glance at each other, do a double take, then break into laughter as they look up into the radiant faces of the parents-to-be.

After dinner Jeff and Russ, Scotch glasses in hand, settle into folding lawn chairs tucked inside the open garage door, sheltered from the east wind blustering off the ocean. Jeff has just told his father about his deployment to Afghanistan. "Don't tell Mom," he says. "No point in worrying her yet."

Russ locks his eyes onto his son's. "Jeff, this is serious," he says, after a long pause, "deadly serious. You and Sylvie are just beginning to make a life together."

"Dad, I'm going there because we have a job to do."

"Then, when you're there," Russ says gravely, "do your job and nothing more. Don't take any risks."

Jeff nods. "I know the first law of combat—don't volunteer for anything."

"And remember the second law: never share a foxhole with anyone braver than you." They chuckle; then sit quietly for a few minutes, watching an osprey circle above the water. It pauses, hovers with beating wings, and plunges feet first, a thunderbolt, into the sea; then rises in a silver spray, a shining fish dangling from its hook claws.

"Jeff, have you ever thought about your own death?"

"Dad, I don't *want* to die," he says, shaking his head. "I won't do anything foolish."

"If anything happened to you, it would kill your mother."

"I'm going to be like the thousand soldiers I go over with. I'm coming back with them."

Russ considers the odds. Between 2002 and Easter 2006, six thousand Canadian soldiers have served in Afghanistan. Eleven have been killed. He feels somewhat reassured.

They talk on, as daylight slowly turns to dusk; twilight time, *the hour between dog and wolf—l'heure entre chien et loup,* the crepuscular hour of metamorphoses. A lone star glints above the grey-blue Atlantic, and the lights of the buoys flicker, green and red.

On May 17, Jeff picks up Sylvie at the airport in Moncton, New Brunswick, an hour's drive from Fanjoy's Point. They're joining the family for the Victoria Day long weekend and the ritual opening up of the cottage—dusting off the lawn chairs, scraping the crud off the barbecue and wading into the chilly lake for the first time. He stows her suitcase in the trunk, then sits behind the steering wheel, immobile, staring ahead at the rows of parked cars. "One of my friends was killed today in Afghanistan," he says. "Nichola Goddard. Hit by an RPG—a grenade—during a firefight."

"Oh, Jeff." She reaches for his hand. "I'm so sorry."

"Twenty-six years old. She has a great husband, Jay."

She remembers him talking about going to their place for a barbecue. "Jeff, wasn't she a FOO?"

"One of the best." He pauses, opens his mouth to speak, but nothing comes out. The first Canadian female soldier to die in combat, he thinks, giving her life for a cause she truly believed in. He blinks back the tears, then turns to meet Sylvie's fearful eyes. "I might have to replace her. I'll be finished my FOO course in two weeks."

They drive in silence. He keeps one hand on the wheel, and one against the small bump of her belly.

Forward Observation Officer Course Report. June 2006. Captain Francis is an intelligent officer, a calm and collected leader, the consummate team player. His ability to assimilate information and apply all lessons allowed him to progress at a much quicker pace than his peers. His performance exceeded the standard. He is a solid leader who inspires confidence in both his peers and his subordinates. He will make an excellent FOO.

When Jeff returns to Shilo after his FOO course, Craig Ethelston surprises him with a welcome-back party. And Jeff surprises everyone there when he beams his announcement: "I'm going to be a father!" Throughout all the handshaking, back-slapping, hugging and congratulating for the rest of the evening, he wears a permanent grin.

During the months of Sylvie's pregnancy, he is immersed in pre-deployment training. He coalesces the airborne team that he—as FOO—will lead for Task Force 1-07, a battle group of over a thousand soldiers based on the Second Royal Canadian Regiment. Thirty-four-year-old Sergeant Clay Cochrane is his second-in-command; Master Bombardier Steve Ker, the LAV gunner; Bombardier Adam Wierenga, the radio signaller; Bombardier Carlo Lajoie, the main driver; and Bombardier David Fradette, backup driver and signaller. All with parachute wings, their party will support the Airborne Company of Princess Patricia's Canadian Light Infantry in Edmonton.

For six months they develop their combat skills through field exercises—staging booby traps, ambushes, minefields and encounters with enemy insurgents. In the classroom, they learn about Afghan customs, culture, politics, insurgency groups; they prepare for the psychological stresses of combat and separation from their families. In their first major training exercise together—Exercise Mountain Warrior—Jeff's team marches for twenty-six kilometres through the swamps and mountains around Hinton, Alberta, pumping water from swamps and creeks through their filters for drinking. They are the only team to make it back on time to the Company RV.

From July to October, they train in CFB Gagetown, CFB Shilo and CFB Pettawawa—in exercises with mythical names: Virtual Archer, Thor's Hammer, Redleg Archer, Spartan Ram, Royal Archer. Their FOO party morphs into a cohesive unit, a tight-knit brotherhood of soldiers and friends. The LAV they'll be manning in Afghanistan has the call sign of G 1-3—it's the vehicle that Nichola Goddard was killed in. The FOO team assigned to the LAV after hers faced heavy combat, but they all survived. So they nickname their team "Lucky 13," hoping that with Nich watching over them maybe they'll be lucky too.

In late October, they travel to CFB Wainwright for the last major exercise, Maple Guardian, a three-week full dress rehearsal with all the units of Task Force 1-07. In the raw wind and snow of the early Alberta winter, the battle group trains for a mission in the stifling heat and dust of the Afghan desert. Soldiers role-play scenarios of Taliban attacks and mass casualty situations in a setting that replicates the terrain and villages of Afghanistan. Wearing authentic costumes and speaking Pashtu, Afghan-Canadians act the parts of the Taliban, Afghan villagers, and interpreters.

At the same time, Jeff is gearing up for the arrival of their baby, whose due date is November 4. His request for leave to attend the birth is refused: "You are the FOO. You can't be replaced if we're in the middle of a critical exercise." On the night of October 26 he gets a distress call from Sylvie. "I had an ultrasound today. The baby is breech, upside down," she sobs. "I have to have a Caesarean. It's scheduled for November 1. I really need you to be here."

"I'll be there," he says. "Whatever it takes, I'll be there."

He knows AWOL has serious repercussions—demoted a rank, assigned extra duties—but so be it. Even before this phone call, he decided he'd be with Sylvie for the birth, no matter what the cost. But the army is more comfortable with schedules. His commanding officer pleads Jeff's case and secures him five days off. On October 31, he removes his uniform and leaves his FOO team to carry on without him in the crucial Afghanistan simulation exercise. Sylvie is waiting for him at the Toronto airport, glowing; her belly as round and ripe as the pumpkins they carved on their first date—thirteen years earlier to the day. Lucky 13.

On November 1, the operating room at St. Joseph's Hospital is overcrowded with emergency C-sections. So it's not until the evening of November 2 that Jeff dons the green hospital scrubs and stands at the end of the delivery table. Numbed with local anaesthetic from her waist down, Sylvie lies draped in pale green sheets, only the smooth mound of her belly lit up in the spotlight. Dr. Simms cuts into her abdomen, down into her uterus. His gloved hand reaches in and scoops out a head, a blood-smeared little face; its nose and mouth are suctioned clear. Then he lifts out the slippery body of a baby boy. He squalls his first cry, and Jeff feels tears wetting his own cheeks. He opens his arms to receive his infant son, gazes into his opaque blue eyes. *Can this little guy really be mine?*

Marion answers the phone that night to hear, "Mom . . . it's happened . . . you have a grandson . . . he's so beautiful," a voice transformed with tenderness. "Ry Logan Secours Francis—born at 8:38 p.m." When she hangs up, she wipes her eyes and checks the numbers she jotted down. *Could it be?* She fishes out Jeff's baby book from the clutter in the armoire, and reads: *Time of Birth: 8:38 p.m.* What are the odds? And another little Scorpio, also born on a day of re-membrance—All Souls' Day, the day for remembering the souls of departed loved ones.

Jeff stays at the hospital and sleeps in a cot beside Sylvie's bed. He gives Ry his first bath, cupping his head of downy dark hair in his hand and stroking warm water over his satiny skin. Whenever it's time for a clean diaper, he says, "Daddy will change the little man." On the second night, Ry is fussing and needs more cuddling to get to sleep. Jeff lifts his head up from his cot. "Can I come into the bed with you two?" he asks. He climbs into the narrow bed, and they snuggle, parentheses around their son. "Sylvie," he whispers. "We have a purpose now. Don't you feel it?"

"Sometimes," she says, "it finds you." The three breathe together, and drift into sleep.

The next day at noon, he has to leave them to fly back to Edmonton. That evening, Sylvie walks out of the hospital with her two-day-old son swaddled in her arms. Her brother and her mother are with them, but she feels bereft. *This isn't right ... Jeff should be here.* A heavy foreboding envelopes her as they descend in the elevator to the underground parking lot. It's the same gut-wrenching stab she felt when the words "It's a boy!" echoed in the delivery room: *Oh my god. This means it might happen now ... and there'll be a little Jeff here, walking around in his place.* A clear, quick, intuitive flare of insight strikes her, but she doesn't want to see. As they drive home through the dark city streets, blaring with sirens and horns, she cries silently in the back seat beside her sleeping son.

Jeff arrives back in CFB Wainwright late that night and saunters into the nearly deserted mess tent. Scott Lang is sitting alone at a table, warming his hands around a cup of tea. Jeff flashes back to their graduation ceremony, and the general's prediction: *At 3 a.m. in some rain-soaked tent, someone will come through the door that you knew from your basic, and you will instantly remember the trials, and feel that instant camaraderie. . . .* He and Scott have been brothers-in-arms from day one, always ending up in the same place at the same time. During their officers' training at CFB Gagetown, Scott brought his wife and kids out for visits to Fanjoy's Point. Now, they also share the bond of fatherhood. Jeff pulls a stack of Ry's pictures out of his pocket and effuses over each one as he lays it on the table. "Probably every parent thinks this," he grins, "but there's just something so special about him—the way he looks at you."

Scott has never seen his friend so loquacious. Jeff never talks about himself; usually Scott has to pry information out of him. "I guess there are other places you'd rather be right now," Scott says, smiling at the photos spread out before him.

"It's like you're torn down the middle," Jeff says. "Part of you is ready, excited about finally going over there. But the other half is worried, and scared, not wanting to leave your family."

Scott removes his glasses and rubs his eyes. "I've been away from my family for about two of the last six years all told. You miss a lot—birthdays, concerts, first day of school. It takes its toll on them too."

"I've submitted a request for a transfer when I return. It will mean a desk job at Downsview. But I'd be able to take Ry with me to the daycare on the base." He chuckles. "It's incredible how quickly your priorities can shift . . . once you feel those eyes looking into you."

November 19 is a cold overcast day in Toronto. Bloated grey snow clouds graze the skyscrapers. After-work traffic is swarming as Jeff and Marion drive to the liquor store to buy some bubbly for Jeff's belated thirty-sixth birthday celebration. The radio news headlines a story on Afghanistan, and Jeff glances over at his mother. "I'm going in February," he says. The words that for months have been lurking like thieves beneath the surface of her mind have finally been spoken—words with the power to steal her son and derail their lives.

"Why, Jeff?" she asks, lips trembling. "Why do you have to do this?"

"It's my job, Mom," he says, pulling into the parking lot. "Those people need help. Do you know what the Taliban are doing to women? Imprisoning them in their homes and underneath those burkas. They're bartered and sold like pieces of property. And children aren't allowed to go to school. The Taliban burn down the schools and kill the teachers."

"But, Jeff, you have your own child to take care of now," she says, eyes brimming, "right here at home."

"Mom, the 9/11 hijackers trained in Afghanistan. This mission is for our tomorrow too."

"Do you know what it would do to us if anything happened to you?" She looks into his eyes.

"Nothing will happen to me," he says, squeezing her hand. "I'll be okay."

In the store, she stares at the blur of sparkling wines and bursts into uncontrollable sobbing. He comes over and puts his arms around her in a great hug.

That Christmas in Eastern Passage, Jeff and his father take six-week-old Ry with them to pick out the Christmas tree.

Jeff insists on going to the same lot on the corner of Windsor and North in Halifax, even though they have to drive across the bridge and contend with the congestion of downtown traffic. It's a tradition, one he can carry on with his own son, who sleeps against his chest in the Snugli as they survey the trees, and load a seven-foot fir onto the roof of the van.

But behind the tree, soon glittering in the corner, and the candles flaming on the mantel, a shadow looms, touching them all. The sound of carols and laughter, the smell of balsam, turkey and sage, can't block out the impending reality of Afghanistan. Only the blessing of baby Ry can lift them up, keep them present, and allow them to rejoice. Home from her teaching job in the Northwest Territories, Mica witnesses her brother's metamorphosis. She watches him soothing Ry when he's fussy, snuggling him onto his shoulder, patting his back. He rocks his son in his arms as he glides back and forth, singing—*Hush, little baby, don't say a word, Daddy's gonna buy you a mockingbird*. If anyone asks to take over, he refuses: "This baby is going to know I'm his father."

By the end of 2006, thirty-six Canadian soldiers have been killed in Afghanistan. In its first combat mission in fifty years, the Canadian military discovers its Achilles' heel: no troop-carrying helicopters. They were sold years ago to the Dutch—who are using them in southern Afghanistan. Hillier's overloaded defence budget can't purchase replacements.

On February 1, 2007, the Lucky 13 team boards the Canadian Forces airbus in CFB Trenton, Ontario—without their leader. Jeff has to fly to England to take one final two-week course for forward observation officers. While he's there, he buys a soccer suit for his son—red shorts, a red-and-white-striped jersey with an All England crest—size 1 2 months. When his tour is up in six months, Ry will be just the right age to wear it. *Just six months,* he thinks, *and I'll be home for good.*

V. GOODBYE

—

When a hero is called for, from a burning building or
on the wine-dark seas, the voice behind the request
is looking for someone to intervene, to overcome
hopelessness, and to beat back the angry, thanatic
forces of the cosmos that appear to be running out
of control. Perhaps what resides at the heart of the
highest definition of the hero is the notion of divinity,
the idea that something greater than ourselves can
create from darkness a guiding and redeeming light.

Bruce Meyer, *Heroes: The Champions*
of our Literary Imaginations

HOW DOES A MOTHER say goodbye—a contraction of *God
be with ye*—to a son who is going to war?

I have tried to picture this scenario, but cannot imagine enacting this ultimate letting-go of my sons. When
the mother of Robert Ross, in Timothy Findley's *The Wars,*
realizes her son has enlisted for World War I, she glares at
him *with Delphic concentration.* Intuitively knowing her son's
destiny, she lashes out in bitter resignation: "I know you're
going to go away and be a soldier. Well—you can go to hell.

I'm not responsible. I'm just another stranger. Birth I can give you—but life I cannot." She and her husband travel in their private railway car to see Robert before he departs for overseas, but she's too numbed by alcohol, too frozen with dread, to go out and say goodbye: "She waved from behind the glass and she watched her boy depart. . . . And this is what they called *the wars.*" Private internal wars accompany the global ones: When a soldier goes to war so does his mother. The umbilical cord is never really severed. It stretches across countries, oceans, continents, even into death's kingdom.

The character of Mrs. Ross helped me understand the story of the young man who would become my father, leaving for World War II without his mother getting up to see him off. *Why didn't she?* I had always wondered. When her nineteen-year-old son enlisted in 1942, my grandmother— Ada Langille Murray—already knew about enduring hardship and the merciless twisting of fate. Born in 1896, she grew up in the Nova Scotia farming community of New Annan where her father, King, was the blacksmith. When he died, his wife, Hannah, and their eight children were left with no means of support. Ada quit school to work on the farm, so that her brothers and sisters wouldn't be sent to live with neighbouring families. They stayed together in their white farmhouse on the hill, surrounded by apple orchards and fields of brown-eyed Susans.

At age twenty, Ada married Kenneth MacLean Murray— "Clain," everyone called him—and moved to the spacious red farmhouse that Clain and his father, Angus, had built at Tatamagouche Mountain. By the time she was twenty-five, Ada had seven children, aged six and under; her twins, Clifford and Pearl, were born thirteen months after her twin girls, Hilda and Hazel. In Ada's twenty-seventh year, just before the birth of her eighth child, Clain was stricken with polio and bedridden for many months. He recovered with a steel brace on his foot, leg and back, and limped around the farmyard with the help of a cane. Not long after, he contracted chronic asthma. So it fell to Ada to manage the farm as well as her household.

She rose with the rooster's crow to milk the cows, then turn them out to pasture. She collected warm eggs from the cackling brood in the henhouse, and was back in the kitchen by six to light a fire in the wood stove, cook porridge, fried eggs, toast and tea—the first of the day's three big meals. After breakfast, she hurried back to the barn to hoist the heavy milk pails and pour a white waterfall into the hand-cranked cream separator. She fed the skim milk to the pigs and calves, washed and sterilized the stainless steel tubs, then churned the thick yellow cream into butter.

Every Tuesday, Thursday and Saturday, Ada baked seven loaves of bread. The flour was ground at the gristmill from wheat they'd harvested; the yeast she made from the hops growing outside the back door. On Monday and Friday, she pulled out her galvanized steel washtub, scrub board and homemade lye soap to hand wash clothes for her family of ten. She hauled buckets of water from the brook behind the house, pulling a cart in the summer and a sled in the winter, then stoked a roaring fire to heat the tub of water. Every night for ten years, she hand washed diapers, for four babies at once after the birth of her second set of twins.

She grew a garden to feed her family for the entire year; stored turnips, carrots, onions and potatoes in the root cellar; canned green beans, peas and corn; pickled cucumbers and beets; transformed strawberries, raspberries, blackberries and currants into sweet jams and jellies. In the evenings, she quilted, or sewed on her Singer treadle machine—soft flannelette nighties and diapers for the babies, matching cotton dresses for the twin girls. She would often be up past midnight, spinning wool from the neighbour's sheep, then knitting it into socks, hats, mittens and sweaters. Some nights she'd be roused by a loud knocking on the door, someone from a neighbouring farm calling on her to midwife the delivery of a baby.

I once asked my grandmother how she had coped with a life that demanded so much of her. "You have no idea," she replied, shaking her head, "no idea." Then she told me a story that clarified why she hadn't gotten up that morning to say goodbye.

One warm summer evening, she had to search in the woods for two cows that had strayed from the herd. She tramped for an hour in the waning light through the tangled undergrowth before she heard their bawling and found them, completely disoriented. She steered them back to the pasture, then hustled for home to wash the kids and put them to bed. Half running, she was halted by a barbed-wire fence. She crawled beneath it and stopped, midway. She sank against the cool damp grass, inhaling the sweet smell of Queen Anne's lace and timothy. She closed her eyes—not wanting to move, or to get up, ever again.

Many years later, on that March morning in 1942, Ada woke before the rooster's crow. A fire crackled in the kitchen. She smelled the porridge Pearl was cooking for her twin brother, Clifford, the bread toasting over the flames, the black tea steeping. She knew Pearl would pack a good lunch for him—thick slices of brown bread with last night's roast pork between them, a wedge of apple pie, a jar of the Jersey's creamy milk. In the shadowy pre-dawn light, she lay there on the straw mattress where she'd given birth to her eight children. The front door squeaked open, then thudded to a close. She felt a chill in the breeze that riffled the flowered curtains, and pulled her quilt more tightly around her—not wanting to move, or to get up, ever again.

Like Mrs. Ross, and my grandmother, and the millions of mothers before and after them, Marion had to say good-bye to her son as he left for a war on the other side of the world—knowing, but trying not to know, that this farewell could be their final one. When Jeff got back from his two-week FOO course in England, he had two days in Toronto with Sylvie and Ry before he left to board the Airbus at CFB Trenton, Ontario. He didn't want his parents, or Sylvie and Ry, to accompany him to the airport. He didn't like good-byes, especially public ones—the paparazzi zooming in, exploiting private moments of anguish.

But the day before he departed, he received a letter.

Jeff, please know how truly proud I am of you and all that you have accomplished. I read about Maya Angelou describing her son as her "monument"—and you are my monument—for all that you are and all that you do, Jeff, I love you. I will be with you each day that you are away—the positive energy force of my thoughts will go out to you over the universe . . . never forget that Jeff . . . love you forever, Mom xo.

———

IN THE MIDDLE OF February, Jeff flies from Trenton to an "unknown" staging area in the Middle East. All deployed troops touch down here at Camp Mirage for two days before heading on to Kandahar. The worst-kept secret in the Canadian Forces, this acclimatizing point is at Minhad Air Base, just south of Dubai on the Persian Gulf. Adjacent to a vast runway, clusters of flat white portables and grey hangars shimmer mirage-like in the middle of the gravelly desert. Around the outskirts of the fenced-in Canadian section, large one-humped dromedaries graze on thorny tufts of grass. A lone acacia tree leans windward, dusty green against a brilliant blue sky.

At this desert base, the only hazards are the searing sun, jumping spiders and snakes. Soldiers eat at a five-star dining hall with exotic fresh fruits and lobster on the menu. They can work out at a well-equipped gymnasium or play beach volleyball. Dressed in their civvies, they can take a bus into Dubai, lounge in deck chairs under fanning palms, float in turquoise sea water—their last chance to chill out with a beer for at least three months.

The camp is a liminal zone, a place in between training—
"playing" at war—and being at war. And like his comrades,
Jeff exists in a liminal state, wavering between fear and anticipation. After the long, hard preparation, he is eager to
put his skills into practice. He has read every book he could
find about Afghanistan—its history, politics and the present
conflict. But an unknown world awaits him, all the trials and
tests of a war zone: *How will I handle the stress of combat? Will
I be afraid? What if I make a bad decision that endangers my crew?
What if something happens to one of them? Or to me?*

Outside the dining hall, he sits in the baking heat at a
picnic table and reads the names his comrades have carved
into the wood. Most of them came back. Some of them
didn't. But he knows he has to return, to raise his son—a
purpose he is surely meant to fulfill. And the words of
Castaneda's Yaqui shaman resurface: "A man goes to knowledge as he goes to War, wide-awake, with fear, with respect,
and with absolute assurance."

VI. AFGHANISTAN

———

Losing yourself, giving yourself to some higher end . . .
is the ultimate trial. When we quit thinking primarily
about ourselves and our own self-preservation, we
undergo a truly heroic transformation of consciousness.

Joseph Campbell, *The Power of Myth*

JEFF STEPS DOWN FROM the Hercules aircraft onto the
Kandahar Airfield. A glaring noonday sun assaults his eyes,
and he pulls his Ray-Ban aviators out of the breast pocket
of his uniform. The NATO base sprawls before him——an
expansive monochromatic maze of brown buildings, tan
tents, grey prefabs, white portables. Dust-covered military
vehicles, ATVs, SUVs and golf carts drone across gravel
lanes. Beyond the walled and wired perimeter, a stony desert
extends to distant craggy mountains——an arid moonscape,
like Luke Skywalker's desert planet at the beginning of *Star
Wars*. Even the few scraggly mulberry bushes and patches
of grass are dull with powdery dust. A parched wasteland
leached of colour, but for the wide cyan sky.

He strolls across the wood-planked boardwalk; wind
whips sand into his eyes and mouth. Diesel smoke fills his

nostrils. He nods to passing soldiers, many with rifles slung over their backs. They wear varied camouflage-pattern uniforms, all with ISAF (International Security Assistance Force) badges, but with different flag insignias on their sleeves—United States, Britain, France, Australia, Romania. . . . Men in khaki shorts and T-shirts play a raucous game of basketball in the square, their shouts and laughter mingling with the roar of engines and the whirr of helicopters. He peruses the boardwalk shops selling carpets, pashmina shawls, lapis jewellery. Familiar signs pop out: Burger King, Subway, Pizza Hut and . . . Tim Hortons. He yearns for the touchstone taste of a triple-triple, and joins the long lineup—*just like at home.*

High-pitched screams resound from the other end of the boardwalk. Skinny barefoot children push and shove each other, rummaging in and around the overflowing garbage bins buzzing with flies. "Where do those kids live?" he asks the Brit in line behind him. "Is there a village nearby?"

"Oh—the garbage kids," the soldier says, craning his neck. "No, they don't live anywhere."

"How do they survive?"

"They're orphans. Most of them don't. "

Coffee in hand, he sips and savours the familiar flavour, ready to head over to Canadian headquarters. The penetrating wail of a siren, then "Rocket attack . . . rocket attack . . . rocket attack" blares around the square. Everyone around him scrambles for cover, scurrying to one of the concrete bunkers. Jeff vaults the railing and dives beneath the boardwalk onto his belly, his duck-and-cover training reflexively kicking in. He knows it's an insurgent missile launch from the surrounding mountains, a daily and nightly occurrence at the base. Most rockets miss the airfield and explode in the desert. But some have crashed in laneways, smashed into buildings—white-hot chunks of metal slamming into walls, wounding soldiers and civilians. Face down, inhaling the earthy smell, he hears the distant thud of a dud missile hitting the ground. A long two minutes until the all-clear sounds. He crawls out of the dark recess, brushes the dust off his uniform. He grins at the large black-and-red sign hanging at the far end of the square:

WELCOME TO KANDAHAR AIRFIELD

A few days later, Jeff and his Lucky 13 team make their first foray outside the wire, outside the relative security of the KAF compound. Their LAV joins the convoy heading west down Highway 1 into the Panjwaii Peninsula south of the Arghandab River. The paved two-lane road is flowing with taxis, mopeds, bicycles, donkey carts, gaudily painted pickup trucks jingling with sparkling baubles, and pedestrians—children, and men talking on cellphones. On this main artery—"Ambush Alley"—IEDs are common. Perched in the commander's hatch, Jeff scans the trees, ditches and mud walls, alert for anything suspicious. His cells thrum on red-code alert: *This is for real. Someone out there wants to kill me.* He watches and waits for the unexpected. Every approaching vehicle and person undergoes threat assessment—a rusty

white Toyota Corolla, a burka-clad figure, an innocent-look-
ing boy. They've all been suicide bombers.

The convoy veers south off the highway onto a gravel
track. They pass lean-tos, ragged tarps ravaged by the wind.
Roaming camels tug on clumps of grass. Carcasses of military vehicles, residue of two decades of futile war with the
Soviets, litter the landscape. Black-haired boys shimmy up
the gun barrel of a rusted tank and swing off the end. These
are children who've known only war; the sounds of gunfire
and bomb blasts have been as familiar to them as the blazing
sun and sifting sand. They shout and wave, and Jeff returns
a smiling salute.

His neck and shoulders are taut with tension, his skin
clammy with sweat under his body armour as they wind up
a jagged mountain trail and reach the summit of Ma'Sum
Ghar. Canadians and the Afghan National Army occupy the
two-hectare forward observation base (FOB), one of the
central posts of Task Force 1-07's operations. Its commanding view of the villages, roads, and river crossings allows
them to monitor the most crucial area of Kandahar province.
He dismounts, removes his two-kilogram steel helmet, and
empties a canteen of water over his dust-smeared face. It's
the longest thirty kilometres he has ever driven.

At six the next morning, he emerges from the fetid tent—
fifty male bodies in a cramped space—inhales the cool
mountain air. The rising sun gilds the brown bluffs with
a copper sheen. The cloudless cobalt sky unfurls like the
wide prairie skies back in Manitoba. Outside the front

entrance of the compound, turban-wearing men with shaggy beards wait to begin work for the day—filling sandbags, emptying outhouses and packing garbage. A mangy feral cat slinks around the Dumpster by the gate. It's calm, even peaceful; just as its Pashtu name denotes— *Ma'Sum,* "quiet," and *Ghar,* "mountain." Then the chopping of a helicopter slices the silence and reminds him why he's here. Today they'll patrol in a nearby village to establish their military presence and secure the area so the provincial reconstruction team and international aid agencies can do their work. He has already observed the results of their efforts—repairs to roads, bridges, schools and irrigation systems.

Jeff and his team march through mud-walled villages that could harbour Taliban cells—most of them do. They tramp down maze-like alleys, their combat boots raising dust along the narrow footpaths. Striding in single file, eyes wary, slowly sweeping a wide arc, they inspect the dirt for wires or signs of tampering, look over the earthen walls, check to the rear, and scan the distance. It's like being in a time warp, Jeff thinks, like stepping back hundreds of years. The low flat-roofed houses made of mud bricks have no electricity or running water. He's reminded of the mud huts his Scottish ancestors lived in three centuries ago.

Old men with brown ancient faces—moulded by sun, wind and war—lean against the sandy walls of the compounds. The bright inquisitive eyes of children stare at him. But there's an eerie absence of women. Sometimes he glimpses one through a small window, a shadowy figure peeking through the screened mesh of a black veil. For them, he knows, it's more like the Dark Ages—forbidden to appear in public without a male relative, routinely physically abused. He thinks about academics with their "cultural relativism" rhetoric, claiming that all social beliefs and customs are equally valid and dependent on the cultural environment. Beam them down from their ivory towers, he thinks, to walk a mile across the scorching sand in a burka.

A month later, in mid-March, Jeff and his crew transfer six kilometres west to Forward Observation Base Sperwan Ghar, a sandy outcrop at the base of the Panjwaii Peninsula. Pashtu for "dusty mountain," Sperwan Ghar was created by the Russians, who trucked in thousands of loads of sand from the southern Registan Desert. Here in the Taliban heartland, their forward observation team will provide artillery support to Princess Patricia's Canadian Light Infantry. As they twist up the gravel road to the FOB, Jeff thinks they could be entering a fort in the Wild West. Thick walls of mud and sandbags, topped with barbed wire, fortify the border. Soldiers keep watch in a lookout tower that flies the red Maple Leaf alongside the black-red-green-striped flag of Afghanistan.

The Lucky 13 team are manning the observation post isolated on the steep summit of the mountain. They settle into their sleeping quarters beneath the OP, a bunk room built into a round concrete reservoir once used for collecting rainwater. They spread their sleeping bags on the green canvas cots lined along the plywood walls. A large

Canadian flag hangs on the end wall; a calendar tacked to another—X's marking off the days. A corner table holds a kettle, tea bags, coffee grinder, coffee beans, bottled water; above it a wooden sign—SPER BUCKS. With electricity and air conditioning, it's deluxe by outpost standards. They call it "the Hotel." Outside the entrance, Jeff nails up a plywood shingle: HOME OF LUCKY 13.

The morning after they arrive, Jeff is loading equipment in the LAV for their patrol to checkpoint five; a vaguely familiar voice calls out, "Oh my god, you look like your father!"

He glances up into the smiling face of a soldier with chestnut hair, the same colour that his was—when he had hair. The years fall away. He's back in a tree fort in the Oromocto woods playing with his two cousins. "Jason?"

"Hey, Jeff, good to see you," he says, extending his hand. "I was wondering when we'd run into each other." Their dads are cousins, both soldiers stationed at CFB Gagetown in the seventies.

"Dad told me that you and Stephen were over here— somewhere," Jeff says, grinning. "It's been a long time. Maybe . . . twenty years?"

"Hard to believe." Jason shakes his head. "Seems like only yesterday we were lining up toy soldiers on the basement floor, eh?" He chuckles. "Now here we are," he says, spreading his arms, "trying to stay alive in this godforsaken desert."

Jeff knows that as a combat engineer, in the most heavily mined country in the world, Jason has one of the toughest jobs in the army. "I don't even want to know how many IEDs you've found."

"This whole fuckin' desert is a junkyard of old Soviet anti-tank mines and artillery shells," Jason says. "And those bastards are rigging them together to make bombs that get bigger and bigger." He looks down at his grimy combat boots. "The really sobering part is cleaning up after a strike."

Jeff appraises his own seventeen-tonne armoured vehicle, then meets his cousin's hazel eyes. "It's good to know that you and Stephen are here. And we'll be on operations together," he says, clapping Jason on the shoulder. "Nothing better than family covering your back."

In the saffron light of dawn, the faint tones of the Muslim call to prayer drift up into the lookout tower where Jeff stands guard duty—*Allahu Akbar, Allahu Akbar.* Surrounded by radar and thermal imaging detectors, he peers through high-powered binoculars at the brown cliffs pocked with caves. But for the eroding force of the wind, the inhospitable mountain terrain has changed little since Alexander the Great crossed it two thousand years ago, and—local legend says—stopped nearby to wash his hair in the Arghandab River. A stone's throw away stretches the Zharey District, the site of fierce battles with the Taliban last summer that killed twelve Canadian soldiers.

Just beyond the outpost's battlements, smoke plumes from a peat fire in the village of Sperwan Ghar. Farmers amble along dirt tracks trodden by centuries of camel trains, on their way to work in fields striped with mud walls and canals from the river. A variegated green patchwork of orchards and vineyards, splotched with squat brown grape-drying huts. The improved security and reconstruction have allowed displaced villagers to re-occupy their homes; children are again attending school. He smiles. The number of Afghan girls being educated has risen from 1 2,000 under the Taliban to 1 . 2 million. He imagines young girls in headscarves opening a book, holding a pencil for the very first time.

Some days he attends *shuras* with village elders—the *jirga*—a council of men with great grey beards and *pagray,* Pashtun turbans wound with ends dangling to their shoulders. In the shade of some mulberry trees, he sits cross-legged with them on the sand and sips hot sweet tea. "*Dersi,* very good," he says, nodding, "*mananna,* thank you." Brown ankles creased with white cracks peek from beneath their loose frayed kameez. He looks into their lined, weathered faces and explains why the Canadian military is here—to help them get on with their lives without Taliban interference. As the translator talks, Jeff wishes he'd spent those eight months of language training in Saint-Jean learning something useful—like Pashtu. The only phrase he understands with any certainty is one that's peppered throughout the Afghan soldiers' conversations: *Insh'Allah,* "God willing," they say, palms turned up towards the sky.

With dark, penetrating eyes, the elders listen to Jeff, and then to his translator, as if they are reading him. Then they talk about the needs of their village: blankets, cooking pots, tarps, a new well for clean drinking water. In heated tones, they complain about the corrupt Afghan National Police, say they don't know who they can trust. "The Canadian military is not here to control or occupy your country," Jeff says, pointing to the flag on his sleeve. "We are here to help you rebuild your village and to keep the Taliban away so you can live in peace. But to do that, we need your help. You need to tell us where they're hiding and where they are planting their bombs."

The men exchange glances, talk amongst themselves; they've heard that the soldiers who wear the red leaf are not like the Russians, or the Americans. "We want your help," the head elder says, "but if you come here too often, the Taliban will make war on our village. They have spies everywhere. In the next village, they killed many men for talking to foreign soldiers and hung their headless bodies from the trees as a warning."

As they explain Pashtu clans and Pashtunwali—their code of honour and fealty to tribal chiefs, their proud warrior tradition—Jeff is again struck with déjà vu. They are so like the stories he's read about his own Murray ancestors and the feuding clans in the Scottish Highlands centuries ago.

One evening in late March, Jeff is lounging against their sandbagged outpost, enraptured by the big blue eyes and toothless smile of his son, photos that arrived today with his mom's letter. He's lost in that other world—Ry's baby bubbles of sound, his soft plump cheeks—when a distressed voice disturbs his reverie: "Just got a call on the radio from the CO at Ma'Sum Ghar," says his sergeant, Clay Cochrane. "They need a LAV over there—pronto."

"Let's wait a bit—see if the call comes in again," Jeff says, tucking the photos into the book on his knee—*Afghanistan: A*

Military History from Alexander the Great to the Fall of the Taliban.

"How are we going to get it there?" Clay asks, starting to figure out the logistics of their route.

"Never mind, Clay. We're not going."

"What do you mean? Aren't you going to call?"

"No. Just ignore it. It'll go away." Ma'Sum Ghar is no more than six kilometres away, but in southern Afghanistan that's an odyssey. The dirt road between the two FOBs, Route Foster, is known as "IED Alley"—the second most dangerous road in the world. In the last twenty-six days, thirteen IED strikes in a five-kilometre stretch of road. *Don't volunteer for anything.* "No point risking the drive unless we have to."

Clay regards him, then sinks down onto a sandbag. "You're right," he sighs.

"Today we drove over an IED that didn't go off," Jeff says, folding his arms across his chest. "One of the engineers told me it was big enough to blast us all into the next world."

"What the fuck . . . ," Clay says with an uncertain smile. "Maybe there is something to this Lucky 13 stuff."

———

BACK IN EASTERN PASSAGE, Marion and Russ live on a precipice. They too survive one day at a time, one hour at a time, until the next news report or phone call from Jeff. Marion tries to imagine him "standing on guard"—even though ten Canadian soldiers have been killed since he's been there, eight from IEDs. Her days and many sleepless nights are consumed with worry over the dangers her son might be facing. With every hourly lead-in to the CBC radio news, her body stiffens with apprehension. She doesn't want to hear, but needs to hear, and wears her radio-MP3 player—a gift from Jeff—whenever she's away from home. One day she is lined up at the checkout in Superstore— "this just in from Afghanistan; two Canadian soldiers killed." Names aren't released. She abandons her shopping cart, rushes home to check further reports on television and the internet, and to call Jeff's base in Shilo. She paces, on the brink of hope and despair, until identities are confirmed.

She spends her days writing letters and collecting items for parcels to send to Jeff and his comrades: boxes of Jeff's favourite nutritional Cliff Bars; beef jerky to tuck in his pockets when he goes on patrol; trail mix, chips, crackers, rice cakes, vacuum-packed dips and salsa; fla-voured Crystal-Lite powder to mask the taste of the water; Starbucks coffee beans and a coffee grinder; magazines— *Men's Health, MacLean's, Military History Quarterly;* sunscreen with the highest SPF; room deodorizers for the sleeping quarters; deodorant, shaving cream, razors, moisturizers, hand sanitizers, skipping ropes; and mini-photo albums of the latest pictures of Ry.

They wait for Jeff's calls by satellite phone from his desert observation post. They scrutinize the tone of his voice and every word for clues. *What is happening? How is he coping?* He doesn't talk about the details of his work or the dangers; doesn't mention his black, swollen eye from falling into a hole during night patrol and getting smacked by his night-vision goggles. He reassures them that he's stationed in a secure area where peace has been restored. They save all his messages from calls they've missed, replay them over and over when they haven't heard from him for a few days: "Hi guys. It's me, just calling to say hi. Everything's good here, couldn't be better. I'll try to call again soon. Love you." The sound of his voice, though fuzzy and faraway, comforts them—*Yes, he has the training, intelligence and endurance to sustain him.*

Darkness hangs over the days—storm clouds of discontent, impatience, foreboding. Especially since Easter Sunday—six Canadian soldiers killed when their LAV struck an IED. Since then, Russ has a harder time convincing Marion, and himself, that their son is out of harm's way. "As a FOO, Jeff stays mainly in his observation post," Russ repeats. "He isn't travelling the roads as much as infantry soldiers." But *six soldiers—all from the Maritimes—in a LAV.* It hits too close to home. They live each day merely to get through to the next, to cross another one off the calendar; determined to push through, to think positively. *Of course Jeff will come home safely; he has to return to raise his baby son.*

In her small condo in Toronto, Sylvie adjusts to a double dose of new reality: a first-time mother with her spouse eleven thousand kilometres away in a country at war. By giving birth, she has been initiated into the powers of life and death; just as Jeff has, soldiering in a combat zone. In the mythic realm of the Aztecs, warriors killed in battle shared a special heaven—*the house of the sun*—with mothers who died in childbirth. And the journey of becoming a mother parallels that of a soldier; it also demands the giving over of oneself to the life of another. Now that baby Ry is safely here, Sylvie faces all the trials of new motherhood, alone. She learns how to care for her infant son; suffers sleep deprivation; soothes a colicky baby, a teething baby, a feverish baby—while longing for Jeff. A static undercurrent of anxiety disturbs her hours, days, weeks and months.

She rocks her nursing son, enfolded in white flannelette; inhales his just-bathed sweetness and finger-curls his feathery wisps of hair. On the table beside them, a bouquet of yellow roses shines in the sinking sun, twelve rose candles. They arrived today, as they do in the middle of every month—*All My Love, Jeff.* Like a pendulum, the rocker glides back and forth, back and forth, marking time, as she waits—again—for her warrior's return.

Fais dodo, colas mon p'tit frère
Fais dodo, t'auras du lolo
Si tu fais dodo
Maman vient bientôt
Si tu ne dors pas
Papa s'en ira.

WITH THE COMING of spring, the Arghandab River swells with rain. The desert morphs to vibrant green in the Panjwaii valley. It's late April when Jeff returns to the Kandahar Airfield to get a flight home for his mid-deployment leave. Late one evening, he walks into KAF's cavernous mess hall and spies Craig Ethelston, eating alone at one of the long wooden tables. "Hey, buddy," Craig grins, their raised fists meeting in their familiar greeting. "You're finally back in civilization. How's it been going out there?"

"It's been a tough month," Jeff says. He chokes up. "Losing six guys on Easter Sunday . . . then two more. Sometimes I wonder if it's worth it."

"You're in the hot spot, man," Craig says. Here at KAF, they have only to fight the rats and snakes; put up with the stench of an open sewage pond and regular RPG blasts. "I can't imagine the stress outside the wire—you guys always on call. And the frustrations."

"But what would it be like if we weren't here?" Jeff asks. In the five years after the Soviets left, the Taliban stoned women to death in soccer fields and created a haven for terrorists. He meets his friend's eyes. "Driving here today, I felt a little more hopeful." He describes the fields they passed— some blooming pink, the colour of the Taliban's cash crop, opium poppies; but a lot more sprouting with wheat, grapes, melons, almonds, apricots; and the reconstructed roads and bridges that enable the crops to be transported to markets.

Craig looks hard at him across the table. "I ran into your sergeant last week when he was here for the ramp ceremony. He said you don't stop—that you're driving yourself into the ground, with no days off for weeks at a time."

"I told my crew that we're in Afghanistan for six months, and we're on duty 24/7," Jeff says. "Besides, my transfer to Toronto has been confirmed. In a few months, I'll be pushing paper around as well as a baby stroller."

"When you return to Shilo in August," Craig says, and grins, "we'll have a big party—a welcome home and a send-off for you."

He'll be back in Shilo long enough to pack up his belongings and clear out of his small apartment in the officers' quarters. Jeff nods and smiles. "We'll have one last tear, do it up really good."

They stroll out into Moon Dust Alley, into the heat of the night. "Stay safe, my friend," Craig says, as they knock their knuckles.

"*Insha'Allah,*" Jeff laughs, holding out his two hands, palms up towards the dark dome of the sky.

———

WHILE JEFF IS ON LEAVE in Eastern Passage with his parents, Sylvie and Ry, Mica obtains four days off from teaching and flies home. A day's travel time each way allows her two days to be with her brother. He downloads all his photos of Afghanistan onto Mica's computer and gives them a virtual tour of Sperwan Ghar, "the Hotel," and the Panjwaii district.

"Progress is just beginning," he says, bouncing his six-month-old son on his knee. He tells them southern Afghanistan is having its biggest agricultural boom in a decade now that irrigation systems are working, and roads and culverts are repaired. He describes sitting with village elders in a room sunk partly underground, sharing a meal of *pulaw*—rice spiced with coriander and cardamom—and building trust. "But it will take time to keep our promises," he says. "If Canada pulls out now, it would be so unfair. Everything that I've said to these people would just be lies."

"How come we don't hear about that stuff?" Mica asks, her eyes sparking. Nothing that gives meaning to the deaths— what's being accomplished—makes the headlines in Canada. To the soldiers, the media's coverage is disheartening.

"If they'd talk about the progress we're making, maybe people would appreciate what we're doing."

"People have pretty simplistic views—war is bad, peace is good," Mica says, looking into her brother's eyes. "The hearts and minds of Canadians need to be won as well as the Afghans.'"

Late one afternoon, a week later, Jeff exits a tattoo parlour in downtown Toronto, LUCKY 13 inscribed above its door. He wears a bandage on the inside of his lower right forearm. His crew decided they would each get a Lucky 13 tattoo while they were on mid-deployment leave. The design— the number thirteen inscribed within a spade, apex point-ing up—was inspired by the spade insignia of an illustrious American regiment, the 101st Airborne Division. He feels he carries a talisman now to protect his men, one that em-bodies the bond of brotherhood they've forged out of the crucible of war. That's why he needs to return. As he spoons cereal into the mouth of his son, or soaps his flying butterfly feet in the bathtub, or curls up with Ry and Sylvie, breathing in their lavender scent, he feels the compulsion to be back there—his men may be in danger. *Only three more months,* he thinks; then he can fall into fatherhood full-time, without duty calling from the other side of the world.

On May 7, towering cumulus clouds brood above the 427 as Jeff and Sylvie drive to Toronto Pearson International Airport. In the back, Ry slumbers in his car seat, wearing the Blue Jays ball cap Jeff bought for him at yesterday's game. Traffic swishes by, cars darting in and out of the passing lane. They wish to slow it all down—time, this drive, this last hour in the cocoon of their black-and-gold Honda.

"Jeff, I know you don't like talking about this," she says, breaking the uneasy quiet, "but . . ."

"Nothing's going to happen, Sylvie."

"I know, but if something did . . . I need to know . . ." She pauses, holding her breath.

"What? If you should find somebody else?" He glances over at her with a tremulous smile. "Yes, that's what I'd want you to do."

"I feel the same way," she says. "If anything ever happened to me, I hope you'd find someone to take my place."

"That would be pretty hard to do, Secours," he says, clutching her hand.

———

WHEN JEFF REJOINS his men at Sperwan Ghar, Clay informs him that the Public Affairs pictures of the team in their tan camouflage uniforms—*in-the-event-of* photos—have gone astray. Clay has orders to reshoot them.

"I've posed for 'the hero shot' once already," Jeff says, turning away, "and I'm not doing it again—a waste of time."

"What is it about having your picture taken?" Clay grins. "In all the photos of our crew, there's a bunch of the five of us together, but none of all six of us—none of you with us."

Jeff walks away. For the next two days, they argue about taking the picture until Jeff finally relents. He stands in front of their LAV, holding his rifle at a downward angle across his torso. He wears his helmet, dust goggles attached. The bright sunlight illuminates the freckles on his flushed face; the dimple in his chin just visible between the straps of his helmet; his eyes half-closed, squinting in the glare; his lips slightly turned up in a smile. The metallic heat of the LAV— fifteen millimetres of hardened steel armour—warms his back as the shutter clicks.

In May and June, temperatures soar to 55 degrees Celsius. When water is delivered to the FOB on the hill, the Canadians joke that it's already the perfect temperature for steeping a tea bag. The Taliban threat is also heating up; summer is their preferred season for fighting. Every time the Lucky 13 team rides out on patrol, they anticipate an attack. In the fertile Panjwaii district, jungle-like fields of two-metre-tall marijuana plants, tree-shaded roads and irrigation ditches create perfect cover for ambushes. Jeff and his crew hump up mountainsides spotted with caves, potential Taliban hide-outs. They slog through swells of white heat, packing twenty kilos of body armour and thirty-kilo rucksacks. They stop to gulp down tepid water from their hydration packs, and

Jeff fantasizes about the big wet snowflakes that fell in late August at the Army Mountain Man competition—on another planet, light years away.

In early June, an intelligence team determines that two major Taliban IED cells have set up in the Panjwaii area. For the troops at Sperwan Ghar, the hunt is on. In the early morning of June 11, a patrol convoy is meandering along the river road on its way back to the base. A deafening explosion rips through the air. The lead vehicle, an RG-31 Nyala, shoots up into a spiral of jet-black smoke, crashes onto its side without wheels or axles. The RG's V-shaped steel hull deflected the blast outward, so its crew escaped with only a few bruises.

That night, on the same section of road, two more vehicles strike IEDs while moving to the site of the explosion. The crews sustain minor injuries. The Taliban are obviously targeting Canadian convoys. The platoons at Ma'Sum Ghar and Sperwan Ghar alter their travel routes and tighten security. On June 19, Charles Company engineers work all day clearing the roads around the two outposts, scanning with metal detectors and setting off small-scale IEDs. Inky smoke trails streak the sky. Small craters from excavated explosives dot the gravel roads.

Just after the sun rose blood red on the morning of June 20, three Charles Company soldiers—Sergeant Christos Karigiannis, Corporal Stephen Bouzane and Private Joel Wiebe—set out in a Gator all-terrain vehicle from a river checkpoint a few kilometres west of Sperwan Ghar. They've loaded up with water and are returning to their section outpost. It's only a kilometre away by the route they normally travel for their daily resupply run. But engineers ran out of daylight yesterday, leaving a section of that road uncleared. Their longer detour will take them north past acres of vineyards, then cross-country to their outpost.

Minutes after the Gator departs, its dust trail still obscuring the horizon, an ear-shattering blast reverberates around the base at Sperwan Ghar. Monstrous smoke clouds darken the skies over the Zharey and Panjwaii districts. Soldiers from the checkpoint rush to the site. A thousand pieces of metal are scattered around a colossal crater in the sand.

The three men felt the ground convulse below them, then booming waves of sound—a blast so loud that their hearts and heads ceased simultaneously. They had no idea what hit them.

When Sylvie answers the phone, Jeff can barely articulate his words: "It's been a hard day. We lost three of our guys."

"I'm so glad to hear your voice. It's been rough here too . . . not knowing. I'm so sorry. I didn't realize they were from your outpost."

"It was our job to ensure that area was safe. We're constantly patrolling, guarding 24/7. The radar detects movement for miles. But they still managed, somehow, to plant that bomb."

"It said on the news that they were in a vehicle that's like a dune buggy. Why were they crossing the desert in something like that?"

"That's how certain we were." He hesitates. "Joel was only twenty-two, just getting started. . . ."

"Jeff," she says, "has anything changed there? Are you in more danger?"

He pauses, and clears his throat. "I'm sure you didn't hear the positive news. A big IED cell was taken down today in the Zharey district—just next to our post."

"No," she says, "only the news that make us pace the floor—until we hear the names. Then we just feel guilty for feeling relieved."

"Remember, the next of kin are contacted before the incident is released to the media. So if you hear it on the news, I'm okay," he says. "I'll be okay—just a couple of months to go, and I'll be back."

He hangs up, nods to the soldiers lined up, waiting to use the phone. He walks around to the back of the building, and kneels down onto the dirt. Above the sandy ridge, a fiery orange ball sinks into a mauve sky. It always takes him a while to recover after calling home—hearing their voices, their worry; and trying to mask his own fears after a day like today. He knows what he's missing, and longs to be there. He has to find again that safe place in his mind where he can leave them, the compartment he unlocks and visits at the end of the day. As he lies in his cot, the snoring medley of his bunkmates in the close air, he enters this room, bright with his treasure of memories, faces and voices. He holds each one up to the light; his wealth of family, his reward for completing this trial. *Fear no more the heat 'o the sun . . . Thou thy worldly task hast done.*

But now he has to pick himself up, brush off the powdery dust and centre himself. He thinks of Bhante, his calm, collected demeanour, his wisdom: *Fear is a delusion of the mind. Just observe it; don't identify with it. Fear of dying comes from a mistaken view of the body—it's not really "me" or mine. There is no self separate from the rest of existence: no proper time to die—it is just your time to go.* Stay sharp, be focused. Be here, now— lives depend on it.

———

AT FANJOY'S POINT, it's not the usual Canada Day week-end of kayaking, playing horseshoes, building a bonfire on the beach and lighting fireworks. Marion and Russ haven't heard from Jeff for several days. They stay within hearing range of the black rotary phone in the corner of the living room, willing it to ring. Marion keeps busy, preparing for Jeff, Sylvie and Ry's visit in August. She paints their bed-room a warm yellow and sets up a crib for Ry; arranges toys, stuffed animals and picture books. Russ hangs a baby swing from a branch of a tall poplar. He puts the mast up on his new sailboat, tests all the rigging, winches and blocks—all set for him and Jeff to hoist the sails for the first time in Grand Lake.

By July 2, it's been ten days since Sylvie—or anyone—has talked with Jeff. When he finally calls, he tells her that he's been in the field constantly on surveillance.

"Something doesn't feel right . . . I'm nervous," she says. "Maybe it's just getting too close to the end."

"It's time to search the real estate listings," he says, "see what's up for sale around the Downsview base. Maybe we should look for a four-bedroom."

"Why four?"

"We'll need one for guests," he says, a grin lightening his voice, "and maybe Ry will have a little brother or sister sometime soon."

Half a world between them, they conjure their sustaining vision—finally a home together, the three of them. They talk about Ry, seven months old today—his first tooth just poking through. "He can sit up all by himself now," Sylvie says. "He loves banging on the pots with a wooden spoon."

"Cool," Jeff chuckles, "can't wait to be there and drum along with him." They talk for forty-five minutes, their longest phone conversation since he's been in Afghanistan. When it's time to say goodbye, she can't let go.

"I don't have a good feeling," she says, choking back her tears.

He tries to reassure her with his motto: "I'm coming back. I'll be home soon."

After the Canada Day celebrations at KAF, the Lucky 13 team returned to their desert outpost on July 2 without their second-in-command. Sergeant Clay Cochrane has flown to Italy to spend his leave with his wife and children. Meanwhile, Major Chris Henderson's infantry company and their partnered Afghan National Army have closed in on the IED cell responsible for the deaths of their three comrades on June 20. Intelligence reports reveal that it's an experienced group of foreign bomb-makers. They could be hiding in Nakhonay, a village east of their post—an area the company doesn't often patrol. Its inhabitants are mainly the Noorzai, a major Pashtun tribe and the most pro-Taliban.

An operation is planned for the early morning of July 4—"to kick the hornet's nest," Major Henderson says— to surround the cell and flush them out into the open. With a combat team of eighty Canadian troops and sixty Afghan soldiers, it will be one of their largest operations. On the night of July 3, soldiers clean their weapons, load magazines, install fresh batteries in night-vision goggles, check explosive bags and mine detectors. As they're organizing their kit, Jeff decides he needs to talk to Major Henderson. The plan is for Jeff's crew to set up an operating post atop Salavat Ghar, a mountain near the village. Equipped with a suite of radios, they will have networks open for communication with ground and air forces—Major Henderson and gunners in the village below, and task force headquarters at KAF. They'll be listening for aircraft roaming the skies overhead, and survey- ing the environs with high-powered field glasses. As artillery FOO, Jeff will call in and coordinate artillery gun support, mortars and helicopter gunships should a fight break out.

"Boss," he says, "I've been thinking about my positioning in the operation tomorrow." He takes a seat across from the major's desk, covered with a relief map of the Panjwaii dis- trict. "If I'm up here on the mountain," he says, pointing on the map to Salavat Ghar, "and there's ground fog in the valley, I won't have a clear view of the village. It'll be tough to pinpoint exact locations of enemy fire if I need to call in some rounds."

The major furrows his brow. "You're right. The valley fog can be pretty thick early in the morning."

"What if I stay with you on the ground and my crew goes up the mountain for observation?"

"That makes sense. Good plan, Captain Francis." Henderson nods. "I should have thought of it myself."

Jeff meanders up the hill to the Hotel and gazes up into the bejewelled sky, awed by the incomprehensible infinity of blinking stars and planets. *All the stars are abloom with flowers.* He thinks about the Little Prince, living and laughing on one of those stars. And about his granny. Which star is hers? He can still hear her soft easy laughter—whenever she told the story about opening her door and seeing him with the two provosts; or about the time they drove Jack's Oldsmobile into the ditch. He smiles, infused with memory.

A meteor flares across the sky. An omen, he thinks, but can't recall if it's for good or ill. Just before he steps down into their bunk room, he feels for the block letters he chis-elled into the rough plywood siding. He traces each letter with his fingertips:

FRANCIS

He carved one letter a week for the past seven weeks— marking his time, leaving his name in the desert. He stretches out on his cot and drops into sleep. A jackal yips and yowls in the distance.

At 1:00 a.m., the soldiers are up, packing gear into the vehicles. As Jeff's crew mounts their LAV, he pounds fists with each of them—Steve, Carlo, David and Adam. "Be sharp up on that mountain, brothers," he says. "See you in a few hours." And he climbs into the back of Captain Matt Dawe's RG-31 Nyala.

At 3:00, the eighteen-vehicle convoy moves out into the pre-dawn darkness and rumbles along the desert track without headlights. Drivers navigate through their night-vision goggles. Intelligence reports warn that the Taliban has put more than eighteen IEDs in the area, so they're taking a route they normally don't travel. It's slow going along Lake Effect Road as thick ground fog obscures the rutted trail.

They reach the outskirts of Nakhonay; infantry soldiers and snipers sneak around to the north end to block an escape route. Engineers and LAVs set up another cut-off on the east side. Then the convoy thunders down the main road towards the village, raising whirlwinds of powdery dust. Tanks, with mine-clearing rollers and ploughs, lead the way. Jeff listens through his crackling headset, ready to call in "danger close" fire support.

A pale sun burns through the fog at 5:30. The armoured vehicles form a leaguer—a circular defensive position with LAV guns facing outward—where a crew will stay behind to operate the radios and weapons systems, and monitor movement in the surrounding mountains. The soldiers dismount, prepare their backpacks and set out on patrol. They troop through the narrow laneways, the village as eerily still as a ghost town, skirt the perimeters of the two walled-in compounds and tromp through the stubbly fields. Patrolling with Captain Matt Dawe, Sergeant Sean Connors and their Afghan interpreter, Jeff feels eyes tracking them.

Two radios strapped to his back, he picks up chatter through his headset: "Taliban are in the area, watching our every move—stay alert."

They come upon some villagers and stop to study them. How would they even recognize a Talib if they met one? Black beards, dark turbans, baggy brown kameez—they just blend in with the locals. Captain Dawe questions them about Taliban hideouts, caches of weapons and bomb-making supplies. The men shrug their shoulders, plead ignorance. But their shifty eyes belie their words. "Yeah, right," Captain Dawe glares at them. "Another fucking wild-goose chase for the elusive Taliban."

They plod on into the pitiless heat of the morning. Traversing an open field, they assess the ground before every footfall. Packed soil is okay. Loosened dirt is suspect. They're halted by a wadi, a gully almost two metres wide rushing with runoff from the Arghandab River. A dog is barking somewhere close by. "How do we get across this?" Sergeant Connors asks, as they stare into the muddy water. "I wonder how deep it is."

"There's only one way to find out," Jeff says, taking a few steps back. He makes a running leap and lands in the middle of the stream. After trudging for two tense hours in the sun—twenty-five kilograms of equipment strapped to his back, twenty kilos of armour encasing his sweating body—this is as good as it gets. He whoops and splashes as the waist-high water swirls around him.

When the major dispatches the order to head back to the vehicles, the mid-morning sun is scorching. There was no kicking down doors and ransacking houses to uncover a bomb-making lab. They are more concerned with showing respect for the villagers and trying to gain their trust. Soldiers strip off their gear, guzzle water from canteens and load up. Jeff's crew and LAV are a couple of kilometres outside the village, so he'll catch a ride back with Matt Dawe. He radios up to Steve at their operating post atop Salavat Ghar. "Just mounting up," he says. "See you guys back at camp." He's about to step into the RG when he hears a commotion around the LAV behind him. Jason is barking one-word commands and gesticulating, trying to round up some Afghan soldiers and steer them into the vehicle. "Master Corporal Francis," Jeff shouts, "having fun?"

Jason turns around to see his cousin's face lit up with laughter. "There's never a damn 'terp around when you need one," Jason calls back, rolling his eyes.

Jeff flashes him a wide smile and disappears into the RG. He pulls the door tight and nods to the men inside the dark steel box. He buckles the seat belt across his torso, settles back against the hard plastic seat and looks around. *The windows are nice, and it's the safest vehicle we've got. But it just doesn't have that secure homey feel of Lucky 13.*

VII. ASCENSION

———

It ended with the linnet, with the birds of turquoise
    color, birds the color
of wild sunflowers, red and blue birds
It ended with the birds of yellow feathers in a riot of
    bright gold
Circling till the fire had died out
Circling while his heart rose through the sky
It ended with his heart transformed into a star
It ended with the morning star with dawn and evening
It ended with his journey to Death's kingdom with
    seven days of darkness
With his body changed to light
A star that burns forever in that sky

Jerome Rothenberg, "The Flight of Quetzalcoatl"

BY 10:30 IN THE MORNING of July 4, it is already heating up to another sizzling day at the Kandahar Airfield. Captain Scott Lang is strolling down the boardwalk on his way to work at Canadian Military Headquarters when he meets a colleague from his regiment. "There's just been another bomb go off," he tells Scott. "We've lost one of our artillery call signs—G 1-3."

G 1-3? That's Jeff. "Lost?" Scott asks. "You mean killed?"

"Yeah—six soldiers dead."

Scott has seen his friend but a few times in the past five months. Jeff was constantly in the field. The last time was on Canada Day—three days ago. They had a beer together, and he noticed the Lucky 13 tattoo on Jeff's forearm. *The last time.* The words sear into his mind. *Impossible.* Jeff's face appears before him—his shy smile, his open infectious laugh. A montage of memories replays in an instant: seeing Jeff cold, wet and miserable during basic training; seeing him hot, sweaty and exhausted in officers' training; seeing him pushed to his limits in pre-deployment exercises. *Seeing Jeff at his worst meant seeing him at his best. I never saw him defeated by anything.*

And in that gut-churning moment, Scott knows what he must do to honour his comrade, what he needs to do to repay his debt of friendship. He marches over to the National Command Element building, headquarters for the Canadian contingent in Afghanistan. He asks to speak with the casualty administrator, the officer who coordinates all aspects of a fallen soldier's return and repatriation. "Sir, I request permission to serve as escort for Captain Francis," Scott says, blinking his eyes quickly to keep the tears down. "I believe I am the best person to carry out this duty, sir." He explains their intersecting career paths, their common circle of acquaintances, their friendship. "The love the soldiers felt for Jeff as a leader and a friend was universal," Scott says, his mouth completely dry as he tries to swallow.

"It would be an honour and privilege for me to escort Captain Francis back home."

The evening of July 5, a pale yellow moon rises above spot-lit Canadian flags drooping half-mast in the warm windless air. Standing at attention on the Kandahar Airfield, Captain Scott Lang feels the day's heat still radiating off the pavement. Six LAVs trundle across the square; six red-and-white-draped caskets protrude from their open hatches. The vehicles come to a stop. Each casket is eased out by eight soldiers in tan camouflage uniforms and sandy combat boots. They hoist the coffins up onto their shoulders and carry them, slowly, along the yellow line of the tarmac between fourteen rows of troops. A soldier bearing a beret in his open hands follows each one. The bagpipes wail into the darkness:

> Amazing Grace, how sweet the sound
> That saved a wretch like me

Scott, as escort, steps in behind the red-and-blue flag of the Royal Canadian Horse Artillery to accompany Jeff's carrying party: three members of his Lucky 13 team, three Sperwan Ghar bunkmates and his two cousins. Their ears brushing the casket; their ashen faces contorted with the burden they shoulder—the body of their comrade, friend and cousin. When all the boots are still, only the flags move slightly in the skittish breeze that has picked up. Row upon row of soldiers stand, heads bowed, berets held over their hearts. In this prolonged pause, the only sound is of muffled sobbing; Scott feels time stop. The world shuts down. Nothing else matters.

"The light that brings life to the world," the padre says, "will never allow the powers of darkness to overcome the light of Canadians like these." He touches on each soldier's life, conjures up their faces, their voices, their strong active bodies—now so silent and still. *"Yea though I walk through the valley of the shadow of death,"* he intones, *"I shall fear no evil."*

The commanding officer calls for the final homage: "Task Force Afghanistan, to your fallen comrades, salute." Thousands of hands dart to thousands of foreheads. A quick formal gesture, Scott thinks, but so leaden with finality. He joins Jeff's carrying party as they approach the greenish-grey Hercules C-130 aircraft—"CANADA" emblazoned on its side. It rests with its cargo ramp down like some great winged beast waiting to receive the fallen warriors into its dark belly. The men carry the silver caskets into the cavity—massive Canadian flags shrouding its walls—and encircle them. They gaze at their comrades' berets lying on top. Internally, they say their farewells.

The Hercules lifts off from the desert, its nose, windowed eyes and finned tail pointing up into the star-studded sky. The warriors ascend, beginning their return—like the mythic Hercules, himself, carried up in Zeus's four-horsed chariot to dwell with the empyreal gods amid the shining stars.

Scott Lang glances over at the two escort officers facing him across the cramped aisle. Only nineteen and twenty-one years old, they sit stiffly in the red webbed seats. Eyes downcast, they appear as numb as he feels. Ears plugged to mitigate the clamour of the Herc's engines, they delve within themselves, engulfed by the duty they have only just begun: bringing their dead friend home to his family and conducting him to his final resting place.

The Hercules touches down at Camp Mirage, and a ramp ceremony again honours the six soldiers as their caskets are borne inside the airport. Scott and his fellow escort officers follow every step, ensuring the coffins are safely secured for the night. Early the next morning, they oversee the ceremonial reloading of the caskets aboard a Canadian Forces Airbus for the flight to Germany. At Ramstein Air Base, ramp rituals again pay tribute to the soldiers as their coffins are carried off the aircraft and laded again the next day. As Scott shadows every movement of Jeff's casket in the four sombre services, he's unfailingly brought to tears by the great respect and dignity accorded his comrades.

The metal-grey Airbus sinks through cotton puffs of clouds, beginning its descent onto Canadian soil. Captain Scott Lang shifts in his narrow seat and steels himself for the repatriation ceremony that's about to unfold at CFB Trenton, Ontario. Wives, mothers, fathers, sons, daughters, sisters and brothers await their loved one's return.

VIII. TEARS

———

For all the history of grief
An empty doorway and a maple leaf.

Archibald MacLeish, "Ars Poetica"

JULY 6. The early morning fog at Eastern Passage lies thick and heavy, merging land, sea and sky into one impenetrable haze. Gerry, a friend of our family since high school, arrives with Tim Hortons coffee and muffins, a big pot of chili he made last night and crusty whole wheat buns. He's also brought the morning newspapers. Marion and Russ didn't allow Jeff's name to be released to the media until late yesterday, so their son's photo and story are front and centre in the provincial and national papers. "It's a good picture of him, Marion," Gerry says, holding up the front page of *The Globe and Mail*.

Her smiling freckle-faced son in his helmet and tan uniform looks straight into her eyes. "Oh, my beautiful boy!" she cries and collapses onto the sofa. His boyish face, his name, his death—on the front page of the national newspaper. *How can this be possible?* She shakes her head, unable to absorb any of it. I sit down and put my arms around her. "When I heard the door open this morning and a man's voice, I thought it was Jeff . . . I thought Gerry was Jeff," she says, shaking her head, bewildered. "I thought Jeff had come home." All I can do is rock her back and forth in my arms—as she cries.

Home they brought her warrior dead . . .
"She must weep or she will die."

So much weeping. "Where can all the water come from?" Marion asks. Streams of salty tears fill the living room; seep outside onto the deck, cascade down the stairs, flow across the road and into the ocean. The high tide rises above the rocky bank, threatening to wash away the houses along Shore Road.

Isis searched the Nile for the body of her murdered husband-brother Osiris. When she found his coffin, she threw herself upon it and flooded it with her tears. Thus, the Nile rises and overflows its banks every summer.

And so the gloomy skies open and torrential rains flood the highway as we drive to the Halifax airport. I'm following behind Marion and Russ's green Mazda van. The military is flying them, along with Mica and Aaron, up to Toronto for the repatriation ceremony at CFB Trenton. My son Gabriel and I are picking up his older brother, Damian, who's flying in from Vancouver. The wipers swoosh frantically on high speed, but we still can't see through the water pouring down the windshield. Like many other cars on tourist-packed

Highway 102, I pull over until visibility improves. His seat in the reclining position, thirteen-year-old Gabriel is curled towards the door, hoodie over his head, earbuds plugged in. He's dealing with death's blow for the first time—witnessing his distraught aunt and uncle, hearing their anguished weeping. His green and golden realm of summer holidays has vanished: he, Russ and Jeff playing navy seals with their Super Soakers in Grand Lake. Up until now, war has been a video game—*Call of Duty*.

Damian emerges into the airport reception area, and I cry with relief and gratitude—guilty gratitude. Twenty-four years old, he's a young man like Jeff in so many ways: a first-born son who has also inherited his grandfather Clifford's reticent personality, gentle demeanour and trademark dimpled chin. Six foot two, like Jeff, he also thrives on intellectual challenges, as he begins his master's degree at UBC this fall. It's been a few years since Damian has seen his cousin Jeff; their summer vacations at the cottage just didn't coincide.

We hurtle down the highway en route to Malagash on Nova Scotia's north coast. To have both my sons safely stowed beside me in our rental car seems as much as I could ask for. "Whenever you say goodbye to someone," Damian says, gazing out the window, "you should remember that it could be the last time you'll ever see them."

The pelting rain changes to showery mists when we turn off at the Folly Lake exit and wind through the green hills of the Wentworth Valley. We stop to buy groceries, and I'm exiting the store when my eye catches the newspaper rack, the Halifax *Chronicle Herald* on top. Jeff stares at me from the front page:

ONE OF SIX SOLDIERS KILLED IN BOMBING WAS OURS

Our family decided to avoid all the media coverage; it was just too painful. But I can't resist picking up the paper and reading about my nephew—his life, and his violent death. Some details are inaccurate—his age, where he grew up—and upsetting: "An unidentified source said Capt. Francis wasn't supposed to be in the vehicle when it went on patrol but offered to help out when a sixth person was needed." *Can this be true?* Shoppers bustle around me with their carts, oblivious to this rent in the universe and the dazed woman, wiping away her trickling tears.

> *Amidst the corpses of her murdered children, Niobe slowly turned to stone—an immense grey rock, weeping an eternal stream of maternal grief.*

Sunlight is shafting through the clouds when we reach the crest of MacLean's hill. Yellow-brown hayfields roll down to an indigo sea. I feel a visceral thrumming in my heart—the landscape of home. On the North Shore Road, across from the Union Hall where my parents met, we pass the house where I lived my first four years. The faded-red house of memory transformed to white vinyl siding and black shutters. Just down the hill, beyond the brook we were forbidden to play in, my McGrath grandparents' house still stands, but with a disorienting facelift as well. White siding covers the pale yellow shingles and green trim of the house that exists more powerfully in my memory. At the end of the lane, a swing hangs from the same branch of the silver maple where our swing once hung. We turn at the carved wooden sign—McGrath Lane—and drive down the rutted lane, through the woods, to our place on the shore.

When my mother, her sister and two brothers inherited my grandparents' property, they divided the waterfront into four cottage lots. They have expansive views of the Northumberland Strait, the warmest salt water north of the Carolinas. My aunt and uncles built their cottages here some twenty years ago. But my mother's land remained overgrown with alders, scruffy spruce and saltwater maples. She was proud, though, to leave the only property she had ever owned—her most valued possession—to her four grandchildren: Jeff, Mica, Damian and Gabriel. When packing up her belongings after her death, we found a picture we'd never seen, tucked away in the back of a cupboard— a framed print of a brown A-frame chalet surrounded by trees. On the back, written in her familiar script:

My little A-Shaped Dream House
I would like to have someday
at my shore lot in Malagash.
May 29th, 1987

This picture now hangs in the travel trailer I parked on her land a few years after her death. Its wide front window faces eastward down the Strait so that the rising sun streams through, summoning me to the day. Every summer I return here with my sons to be nurtured by the sea and by land that remembers me. And every summer, Marion and I take a few more steps towards realizing our mother's dream, to build a place that's rooted in the soil from which we grew—for our children, and grandchildren, and great-grandchildren. . . . The building site is prepared, waiting for the cottage that we planned to have constructed this summer. But now, all has changed . . . *changed utterly.*

Throughout the humid afternoon and evening, my sons dig into the red dirt and hack through the matted tangle of tree roots to make horseshoe pits. Dripping with sweat, they haul bucket after bucket of sand up from the shore and wheelbarrow it into the one-metre-square depressions. After a cooling swim, they still have enough daylight to throw their first shoes. I sit on the bank, inhaling the salty air, hearing thuds in the sand and occasional clinks on the iron stakes. The lights of Prince Edward Island blink across the water. Three hundred metres straight out, a reef stretches under the sea—shallow enough at low tide that my father would swim out during the off-season, hauling a lobster trap.

A solitary blue heron spires on the rocky shoal. Waves foam with lacy flounces, breaking and receding, the eternal sound of breathing, the ceaseless ebb and flow. Through eyes blurry with tears, I see Jeff sauntering down the sandbar in a white tank top and knee-length shorts. He wades through the lapping waves, his muscular body silhouetted against the violet and crimson sky.

IX. FIFTY BRIDGES

———

I'm not a bird but I'm inhabited by a spirit
that's uplifting me. It's my animal, my saint
and soldier, my flame of yearning,
come back to tell me
what it was like to be without me.

Chase Twichell, "Saint Animal"

JULY 8. At the entrance to the CFB Trenton airfield in southern Ontario, wreaths of red and white carnations hang from a chain-link fence. Six large Canadian flags sag from the ends of poles planted in the dry grass. On this hot, muggy afternoon, people line the fence, wearing red and white clothing and clasping Canadian flags. Reporters, cameras slung around their necks, are perched on stepladders, zoom lenses poised like cannons above the barbed wire, ready to shoot.

Inside the passenger terminal of the airport hangar, the families of the six soldiers are waiting. In a brightly lit room that smells of coffee, tables are covered in white cloths and heaped with platters of sandwiches and sweets—that no one appears to be eating. People with blank expressions sit on the edges of the cushioned chairs that circle the edges of the room. Men in dark suits and women in black skirts and dresses stand in small clusters, looking lost—as if they've come to the wrong party and don't know what to say, or how to leave. Russ wears his congenial face as he meets members of the other families, attempting to normalize what is totally abnormal. He can't think about why he is here.

Mica stays close to Aaron, fidgeting with her bracelets and rings. She tries to smile when people shake her hand; her face rigid in a frozen mask when the Governor General's representative says, sotto voce, "Thank you for your sacrifice." *What does that mean?* Just four days ago, she was laughing in a boat on the edge of the Pacific. A second later she was flung overboard. She is still just treading water, knowing there's no one to rescue her. This is her life now, merely trying to survive and support her parents. July 8—her thirty-second birthday.

Down the hall, in a narrow unlit room, Marion sits—alone. She stares out the window overlooking the runway, rebuffing the pressure to socialize, to make small talk with strangers while she awaits the body of her son. *Impossible.* The ache in her heart is all-consuming. The plane is late. They've been waiting for over an hour. Just as they waited all morning at the hotel in Toronto, waited and wondered how they would endure the hours. Waited and walked, pushing Ry in his stroller through the crowded city streets—streets full of young men, fathers holding the hands of toddling boys. They walked and cried, walked and wondered how they'd get through it, terrified.

The plane's imminent arrival is announced. The families are directed to queue up in order of the soldiers' seniority—the protocol of military hierarchy observed, even into death's domain. Jeff's family goes out first, out into the heavy humid greyness of low-hanging clouds. Twelve black limousines are parked, twelve black-suited chauffeurs beside them. In front, six hearses, sleek and black as sharks, wait. Assembled in parallel groupings, the families stand mute, tracking the grey Airbus as it touches down and taxis in. The cacophonous motors and whirring turbines shut down. They all fix their eyes on the cargo door, just behind the front wheels, anticipating the moment none of them wants to witness—when the hatch opens and the bodies of the men they love emerge, encased in aluminum. A young woman rocks a crying baby in her arms. A small golden-haired boy in a green plaid shirt holds his mother's hand and waves a long-stemmed yellow rose. "Bye, Daddy," he calls, staring at the airplane.

Sylvie snuggles Ry close in her arms. In a red-and-white Canada Day T-shirt, gurgling and grinning, he looks around at all the faces. Through her sunglasses, she scans the men in their tan uniforms, wondering where her soldier is, aching for Jeff's arms around her. When she returned to her condo this morning to pick up some clothes, a dozen yellow roses lay on her back step—*All my love, Jeff*—wilting in the sun. And she felt a surge of strength—*he's still here, somewhere*. But now she has to go through the motions of this ritual, gripping this yellow rose for him—for his coffin that's about to come out of that plane. She doesn't believe he can really be in there. She wonders why this band is playing, and when she'll wake up.

A bagpiper—in beaver hat, gold-braided navy jacket, green-black tartan kilt—pierces the still air:

> I've heard the lilting, at the yowe-milking
> Lassies a-lilting before dawn o' day;
> But now they are moaning on ilka green loaning
> The Flowers of the Forest are a' wede away.

Out of the dark cavity, the first flag-covered coffin comes into view; Captain Jeff Francis lowered to the ground, repatriated. Captain Scott Lang stands on guard. Eight soldiers in dark green dress uniforms march forward. With black-gloved hands, they lift the casket onto their shoulders. Their linked outstretched arms form a bridge for it to rest on, as they carry it to the open hatch of the hearse.

Marion knows that this is the moment they're meant to walk across the tarmac. Numb, she puts one foot in front of the other, one black sandal following the other. She wades through dense waves of heat. Her gauzy black cotton skirt brushes her bare legs. Russ's shiny black shoes follow in step beside hers. In a dark blue suit, he holds a yellow rose upright in one hand and clenches her arm with his other; his eyes set with the grim necessity of undergoing this surreal ceremony: *Be strong; guide and support Marion. Don't think about what is actually happening here. Deal with the emotions later.* Their moist hands interlocked, they approach the rectangular box wrapped in red and white. Marion embraces it, the cotton flag and aluminum casket cold against her cheek—*Jeff, you've come back.* Her physical closeness to her son's body brings her relief and release—*you're with us now. You've come home.*

This tableau unfolds five more times, for the families of

Captain Matthew Dawe
Master Corporal Colin Bason
Corporal Jordan Anderson
Corporal Cole Bartsch
Private Lane Watkins

Three police cars, overhead lights flashing, lead the motorcade out of the airfield. The families in black limousines follow the six black hearses. The streets are packed with people, dressed in red and white, waving Canadian flags, holding up signs:

WE SUPPORT OUR TROOPS

THANKS FOR OUR FREEDOM

WE LOVE YOU

Veterans, in navy berets and medal-bedecked blazers, salute with knowing eyes—*there, but for the grace of God, go I.* Children in white T-shirts wave small plastic flags. Hands over their hearts, firefighters stand rigid on the roofs of their engines, huge Canadian flags flying from the tops of the extended ladders.

The procession winds onto the highway, a serpentine stream of headlights. Passing motorists honk their horns and blink their lights. As the motorcade converges on the first overpass bridge, splotches of red and white stand out against the concrete and misty grey sky. Canadian flags drape the length of the bridge. Throngs of people clad in red and white line the railing and spill over onto the grassy edges. They stand, shoulder to shoulder, leaning on one another, wiping their eyes, waving flags, hats and hands—a sea of red and white.

At the second overpass bridge, the same ovation greets the motorcade—and at the third bridge, and at the fourth . . . past exits to Brighton, Grafton, Cobourg, Port Hope, Oshawa, Whitby, Ajax, Pickering—all the way to Toronto. As the fallen young men pass under the arches of fifty bridges, they are lauded by thousands of flags and thousands of people, young and old. They have stood for an hour on this sultry evening, watching for the headlights down the 401, waiting to pay their respects to the soldiers and their families. And between the bridges, all along the 172-kilometre route, police officers and firefighters in full-dress uniform, ambulance drivers and paramedics stand in salute beside their vehicles.

With every bridge they pass under, Marion, Russ, Sylvie, Mica and Aaron gaze in wonder. The sentiment emanating from the crowds penetrates the tinted windows of their limo. They grasp each other's hands as tears of gratitude mingle with their tears of sorrow. They never expected such an outpouring—this benediction—during this interminable two-hour journey. It's the first time such multitudes have inundated these fifty bridges—the route that would soon be officially designated the "Highway of Heroes." The weight of their grief—from the French word *gref,* meaning *heavy*—is lightened, as it's borne on the shoulders of Canadians. Ordinary people acknowledging their debt, the price that these soldiers and their families have paid on their behalf: *The dove is never free.*

The setting sun paints rosy streaks in the saffron sky as the grey city towers rise up in the distance. On the outskirts of Toronto, the overpasses span a dozen lanes. They too are curtained with Canadian flags and teeming with people, red and white from end to end. The entourage turns off at the Don Valley Parkway, continues south to the Bloor Street exit and into the neon-lit streets of Toronto. Red Maple Leafs hang from the lampposts. People line the sidewalks, flourishing flags, all the way to the coroner's office—the hearses' final destination.

———

JULY 9. Captain Scott Lang sits alone at the front of an Air Canada Boeing 777. He boarded early, after the private ramp ceremony for the loading of Jeff's casket. On the window seat beside him rests a kit bag, packed with Jeff's beret and all the items Jeff carried in his pockets during his final operation. Beside the brown leather bag is a black wooden box with a glass face—the shadow box for the flag covering Jeff's casket. He puts a protective arm across them, knowing that during takeoff he'll have to stow them beneath the seat. As passengers begin to stream past him down the aisle, he closes his eyes, breathes in the cool air whistling through the vent. He broods over the upcoming stage of his duty: accompanying the seventh and final ramp ceremony at the Halifax airport; securing Jeff's casket at the Dartmouth funeral home; inspecting every detail of Jeff's uniform before the family viewing—all the while remaining in the background, respecting the family's privacy.

As the plane taxies down the runway, a bass voice sounds over the intercom: "Ladies and gentlemen, this is your captain speaking. I'd like to inform you of the special circumstances of our flight to Halifax today. As pilot, I have the honour of flying home the body of Captain Jeff Francis, killed in Afghanistan on July 4. The soldier seated at the front of the aircraft is Captain Scott Lang, serving as escort for Captain Francis."

Escort—such a benign term, Scott thinks as he shuts his eyes to the glances of passengers seated around him. He has grown accustomed to being treated like royalty with leprosy—*everyone knows you have an important role, but nobody really wants to talk to you.* He presumed this duty would be tough—bringing his dead friend home, seeing Jeff's family broken with grief. But he couldn't have imagined how tough: the accumulation of many small tasks, solidifying into the single hardest thing he's ever done.

July 9, Eastern Passage. Just before noon, my sons and I arrive back from Malagash. The blue Atlantic spangles with sunlight. But the house on Shore Road is cold, empty and lonely. The sorrow of its occupants has seeped into the walls and furniture, hangs in the flower-scented air. Luxuriant bouquets—white lilies, red roses, purple delphiniums, delicate baby's breath—fill the living room, their fading blossoms scattered on the tables and floor. *The flowers of the forest are a' wede away.*

Anticipating my family's return from Trenton this evening, I clean the house upstairs and down, open all the windows to let the ocean breeze blow through, and water the wilting plants. I make a green salad and garlic bread, heat up Gerry's chili and a seafood casserole brought over by a neighbour. As dusk creeps in, I light candles in the living room and dining room, turn on the outside lamps. The sun sets a fiery blaze in the sea and sky as their van pulls into the driveway.

I embrace my sister. Her body feels frail and hollow. "We got to hug Jeff's coffin," she sobs. "He'll be home soon." I shudder within, think of my own sons, and find that I'm unable to go there—to that place of horror. A curtain drops over the inconceivable.

"I know this isn't a time for celebrating birthdays," I say, popping the cork on a chilled bottle of Henkel, "but I want to toast Mica. I'm so glad you were born thirty-two years ago." Her face pallid against her long dark hair, she smiles as I pour the bubbling wine into her fluted glass.

"I still can't believe I forgot your birthday yesterday," Marion says, shaking her head.

"It's okay, Mom," Mica says, tears welling in her eyes. "Getting this present from Jeff was all I needed." She strokes the arm of her chocolate-brown lululemon hoodie. "Jeff bought this when he was home on leave, and left it with Sylvie for my birthday," she tells me with a thin smile. "Mom said that whenever I wear it, Jeff will be giving me a hug."

After dinner, we talk about seeing Jeff's body, one last time, at the funeral home in Dartmouth, a private viewing for our immediate family. Considering the violent nature of his death, we didn't think we'd have this opportunity. So we're grateful for this small mercy, but also apprehensive, afraid we may not see Jeff as he lives in our minds, that death's hand will efface our memory bank of images. I flash-back to my first and last visit to a funeral home. Thirty-nine years ago to see my father, who didn't look like my father at all. The artificial beige skin, rouged cheeks; lips that were too full, too red; eyes sealed shut. The cleft was still there in his chin, but I knew my father was elsewhere. His body like an empty shell left on the sandbar by the outgoing tide.

"I have to see his body," Sylvie says, wiping her eyes. "I have to see him. Maybe I'll believe it then, that this is real. We were apart so much. It feels like he's just away. But I'm not sure about taking Ry."

"Why wouldn't you?" Marion says, meeting her gaze.

"I'm just not sure how it would affect him," Sylvie says.

"But it's his father," Marion says, leaning forward in her chair.

Sylvie lowers her eyes, and sits in stony silence.

July 11. Early in the morning, Marion and Russ leave for Dartmouth. They stop for coffee next to the funeral home and order a triple-triple to take for Jeff. They enter the cool hush of the viewing room. A framed photo of Jeff sits on one table, a bouquet of red roses on another; in between, a half-open wooden casket draped in the Canadian flag, Jeff's green beret on top. It's been a week since he died, so even the mortician's art can't disguise the mask of death. But his parents can see beneath it—to the face of their beautiful boy, his dimpled chin, his faint freckles, his smooth shorn head. In his tan camouflage uniform, he lies in folds of white satin. Marion requests that the coffin be opened all the way, so she can see and touch all of her son's body, down to his feet inside his combat boots. Russ embraces him, cold like no other cold, tries to cradle his son in his arms one last time, but he can't lift him—his body is too heavy.

A few hours later, Damian and I drive the coastal road to the funeral home. A cornflower-blue sky, a calm sea coruscating with sunbeams—so much light and beauty on such a dark day. When we walk into the stillness of the viewing room, Marion asks us to stay back several feet from the casket where chairs are arranged. "You'll be able to see a truer likeness of him," she says. "This is what Jeff would want." With his shaven head and peaceful repose, he looks as he did in the cradle, deep in his newborn sleep.

We sit in a semicircle around him—Sylvie, Marion, Marilyn, Mica and I—trying to absorb the reality of Jeff's transformation. *This is the body that he has left. But the essence of Jeff is elsewhere—in the very air we're breathing.* Sylvie stares in shocked disbelief, dabbing her puffy red eyes with a Kleenex. Lost in the dense woods of memory, we feel a tranquility enveloping us, a serenity so complete that our eyelids grow heavy, somnolent.

Russ comes in, carrying his grandson who has just wakened from a nap in his stroller. As Russ approaches the casket, Ry looks at his father's body and raises his hand in a high-five gesture. It's a way we often greet Ry: "High-five!" And he grins and slaps our open hands. Russ turns and regards us, thoughtfully. "Sitting here with Jeff," he says, eyes tearing up, "are the five women who loved him best." He passes Ry to Marion and hugs us each in turn.

Mary Magdalene, Joanna, Mary the mother of James, and Salome go at sunrise to the tomb where Jesus was laid, bringing fragrant spices and perfumes to anoint his body. But the stone has been rolled away, and the body of Jesus is gone. Two white-robed figures appear. "Why seek ye the living among the dead," they say. "He is not here, but is risen."

———

SCOTT LANG EXITS THE crematorium. Under his arm, he bears a hand-sewn, thickly woven Canadian flag—the highest-quality flag, reserved for prime ministers, Governors General and fallen soldiers. Bleary-eyed, he drives slowly across the Murray MacKay Bridge, and through the tree-lined streets of Halifax. He pulls into the driveway of his sister-in-law's home where his wife is staying. She has come from Moncton, New Brunswick, to support him through these draining days. "Cara," he says, when she meets him at the door, "I need your help with a very important job."

They each hold one end of the outstretched 1½-by-3-metre flag. They fold it in half lengthwise, then in half lengthwise again. Scott brings his end forward over his hands four times, leaving one point of the scarlet leaf against the white background. As he folds, he thinks about the colour of blood, stark against the colour of innocence. He is seeing everything now in a different light—his job, his family, his priorities. It's as if a filter has shifted.

He lays the flag in the shadow box and clicks its glass cover shut.

JULY 12. Leaden clouds hang over the grey ocean, churning with whitecaps, as the dark green car pulls into the driveway. The morning has been heavy with nervous anticipation, as we waited for this delivery—this next stage of facing what is still unreal. In his camouflage uniform and combat boots, Captain Scott Lang lumbers up the stairs, cradling a small wooden chest in his arms. Marion and Russ go outside to meet him on the deck. Scott passes the urn into Marion's outstretched arms. She crosses the threshold into the house and looks at us, frozen in our chairs. "This is my son," she says, tightening her embrace of the smooth mahogany vessel.

Scott takes a seat on the couch within our circle. His eyes brim through the lenses of his wire-rimmed glasses as he presents the family a large picture frame, wrapped in white tissue. "This is a photo that none of us like posing for," he says. "No one is ever smiling because we know there's only one reason our family would ever see it." In the 60-by-90-centimetre photograph, Jeff stands in front of the Canadian flag in his green uniform and beret, the RCHA badge over his left eye. His hazel eyes are liquid and averted; his down-turned lips project a remorseful awareness of the magnitude of *this moment*. It was taken at CFB Shilo in January, a month before he deployed to Afghanistan.

Scott then opens a square wooden box containing items that Jeff carried with him at the time of his death: a pocket knife, the silver watch he received as top candidate in officers' training; a small bottle of sunscreen Marion had sent. His fair freckled face burned so easily; she always nagged him about applying sunblock, and he always humoured her—*Sure, Mom*. But there it was, in his pocket, along with Sylvie's St. Christopher medal and the shiny green pouch with the protective gems she'd sent. She unties the draw-string and lets the stones spill into her hand. Two are broken. "Shattered," she says.

We choose July 17 as the date for Jeff's memorial service: 17-07-07, synchronous with his birth date—11-11-70. The multiples of ones, sevens and zeroes emphasize the significance of each number. The service will be private—Jeff's wish, to have the intimate bonds of his family, close friends and comrades. Moreover, we want to avoid the scrutiny of the media, who feed like vultures on death, turning people's suffering into a spectacle or sound bite. The Reverend Jane Doull, Minister of the United Churches in Wallace and Malagash, makes the two-hour drive to Eastern Passage and spends a morning talking with us about Jeff, his spiritual path, and the format for his service: *Jeff's Time of Remembrance*. She suggests many Buddhist texts for readings, and leaves us feeling confident she'll prepare a service that honours Jeff in the spirit of his beliefs.

We dig out stacks of albums and boxes of photos. Marilyn and I assemble collages to display in the reception hall, a kaleidoscope of Jeff's life: from chubby, laughing babyhood to freckle-faced, shy boyhood; from hipster-punk adolescence to shorn, muscular manhood. Every picture has a story, and we remember—Jeff running away to Granny's house, Jeff committing his "dastardly deed"—and we laugh, and cry. Marilyn's husband, Mike, burns CDs of Jeff's favourite songs to play in the background during the gathering at the Wallace Community Hall. Mica and Aaron design the memorial leaflet with photos and verses, and arrange for the printing. Sylvie spends hours at the computer, booking airline reservations for family members travelling from across the country—Air Canada providing complimentary first-class tickets.

Russ oversees the logistical details of the service and the reception, and he drafts a eulogy, stoically in control during the day. But at night he clings to his daughter's arms, crying: "I love him so . . . I miss him so." Marion also writes a eulogy for her son. "I have to do this for Jeff," she repeats, papers and books spread out before her on the dining room table.

She reviews philosophical texts that guided him, and quotes passages he underlined in his dog-eared copy of *The Art of War* by the Chinese warrior-philosopher Sun Tzu: "The Art of War wars against war. And it does so by its own principles; it infiltrates the enemy's lines, uncovers the enemy's secrets and changes the hearts of the enemy's troops."

And I compose my tribute, its seeds sown during my eight-hour flight from Kelowna to Halifax. As I pondered Jeff's journey, from his birth on Remembrance Day 1970 to his death on Independence Day 2007, I gleaned mythical underpinnings: abandoning his Ph.D. and becoming a soldier culminated a lifelong search for purpose, his quest and his destiny. When I pulled *The Power of Myth* from his bookshelf and skimmed its pages, I could see in the many passages he'd highlighted, his own story: *The myths help you read the messages of the world.* Perhaps his death wasn't random or senseless—"a bit of bad luck," as his commanding officer phrased it. I hope that this story of Jeff's life—the hero's journey—will provide some sustenance for our family. A story can be as essential as food and water in restoring people to life.

And through the week of preparation, sweet baby Ry keeps us going, lifts us from unabated sadness into moments of joy. As we walk and rock him, feed and diaper him, bathe and dress him, we delight in the satiny softness of his skin, his dimpled knees, his snuggly hugs. Gabriel plays on the floor with his little cousin and carries him around if he's fussy. When he reads him his favourite story, *The Barnyard Dance,* Ry flaps his arms and kicks his chubby legs. "I didn't know I liked babies so much," Gabriel tells me. We assemble a montage, photos of Ry juxtaposed with baby pictures of Jeff. If it weren't for the faded colours in the images of thirty-five years ago, you wouldn't know one from the other. But the happiness Ry bestows is "bittersweet," as Marion puts it. "Just look at what Jeff is missing," she says, tearfully shaking her head, "and this little boy . . . will never know his daddy."

———

July 17. The mid-morning sun illumines a slate-blue sea, and waves sough along the granite-banked shore. Six cars, with Canadian flags fluttering from their aerials, set out from Eastern Passage. Marion and Russ lead the procession, Jeff's urn nestled between their seats. Following close behind are Captain Scott Lang and Captain Jason Chetwick, Sylvie's assisting officer—her liaison with the military, and all-around support provider. Trailing their green sedan are four cars, members of Jeff's Murray-Francis-Secours family making this final 170-kilometre journey with him.

Driving north on the hectic four-lane freeway, we pass a large blue sign, a poppy in its upper right corner, and white lettering:

Veterans Memorial Highway
Lest We Forget

At Truro, we turn onto single-lane Highway 311, edged with red dirt and ditches luxuriant with Queen Anne's lace, purple vetch and red clover. We wind through the forested Cobequid Mountains, the land our Murray ancestors settled, and memory-inducing place names appear: Sutherland Road, Rogart Mountain, Earltown. Just east of the highway in the Scotsburn cemetery, the graves of Jeff's great-great-great-great-great-grandparents lie beneath the spreading branches of a massive sinewy oak. The chiselled letters on their granite slab tombstone, imported from Scotland, are still discernible beneath the crusty lichen:

In Memory of William MacIntosh
Native of Parish of Rogart
Sutherlandshire N.B.
who departed this life 27 April 1835
and
Christy Murray
who departed this life 27 June 1863
Aged 102

We pass the sign for New Annan where our grandmother Ada's family home remains, a white farmhouse surrounded by apple trees and meadows blooming with golden glow. At the junction leading to The Falls, a boarded-up church with peeling white paint adjoins the cemetery where Ada and Clain lie beside Clain's parents, Angus and Joanna—"Perpetual Care" engraved on their tall sandstone monument. If we were to take the road to The Falls, we'd soon arrive at the Murray farmhouse where our cousin now lives, the site of our annual family reunion.

By noon we reach Wallace, a sleepy seaside village that's changed little since the fifties. Our aunt Pearl lives here—aged eighty-five, the sole survivor of the eight children Ada birthed. Pearl and our ninety-one-year-old uncle Millard live on Wallace Bay, a few steps from the wharf stacked with lobster traps and ringed with fishing boats. We stop at the community hall to set up for the reception. In the twenty-five-degree heat of this windless day, the odour of dried fish and seaweed are pungent in the low tide.

My black sleeveless dress has no pockets, so I toss my car keys into the compartment between the seats, and close the door. I carry photos, collages and flowers into the hall, then return to the car to retrieve my purse. The door is locked. My stomach sinks. All the doors are locked, all the windows rolled up. I spy the only key inside, shining silver in the sun. Two leather handbags lie beside it; mine with my tribute tucked inside, and Marilyn's with the verse she's going to read. In the locked trunk are six baskets of red and white carnations to adorn the gravesite. The service begins in an hour.

Aaron sprints down the street, around the corner to the RCMP station. The local expert in car break-ins arrives in ten minutes, a white-haired man who inspires confidence with his greasy bag of specialized tools. He works for fifteen minutes, then scowls, stymied by the latest anti-theft technology on my rental Chevy. We have half an hour to get to the cemetery for the 2:00 service. Captain Jason Chetwick, looking cool and in-charge in his green dress uniform, whips out his cellphone and makes two quick calls. Within minutes, a tow truck is on the way.

Meanwhile, I am frantically scribbling on a piece of paper laid against the hot metal of the car roof, trying to stifle the panic, focus my thoughts, jot down the main points of my Hero's Journey tribute. Everyone mills around the car, waiting and watching down Wallace's main drag for a tow truck. "I'm so sorry for creating all this stress," I say to Marion, "as if you didn't have enough to worry about."

"It's okay," she replies, with unexpected calmness. "We can just break the window if we need to." The men dart glances at each other, aghast at this suggestion. But she's right; she knows what's important now. Within fifteen minutes, the tow truck arrives, and five minutes later the door is unlocked. We pile into our cars, buoyed by the synchronicity of the timing. "Jeff never liked all the attention to be on him," Marion says, with a small smile.

At exactly 2:00, we drive up the hill to the Wallace Cemetery. It's hot and humid, but a salty zephyr blows up from the Strait, rustling the leaves of the birches, wafting the scent of buttercups, daisies and wild roses from the grassy border. Next to the black granite headstone of Jeff's granny and his grandfather-namesake, a hushed crowd awaits our arrival: Grandfather Francis, aunts and great-aunts, uncles and great-uncles; Murray, McGrath and Francis cousins; friends from near and far, comrades from CFB Shilo. The gravesite blooms with red geraniums, purple pansies, wreaths of white lilies and red roses, red and white carnations—all enclosed by Canadian flags.

The bagpipes call from higher up the hill, their heart-rending cry keening over two centuries of tombstones:

And so this soldier, this Scottish soldier
Will wander far no more and soldier far no more
And on a hillside, a Scottish hillside
You'll see a piper play his soldier home

We form a semicircle behind the podium, our arms inter-locked, clammy hands clutching our papers. Out beyond the congregation, snow-white gulls wing above the pale blue expanse of Lazy Bay. "We have come together to honour Jeff's life and his spiritual path," Reverend Jane begins. "He was a deep reader, a thinker, a seeker, someone who sought to live an authentic, meaningful life, and to love and serve this world in the best way he could."

A yellow Support Our Troops ribbon pinned to the lapel of his jacket, Russ walks up to the podium. With his grey handlebar moustache and erect bearing, Major Francis is just below the surface. But his military medals are not on display today. He is a father who's lost his only son in an occupation that he, himself, survived. "Jeff felt a strong connection with animals and nature," Russ says. "Several years ago when we lived on Williams Street in Halifax, birds often flew into our dining room window. One day, a baby crow crashed against the glass and fell to the ground, unmoving. Jeff rushed out and found that its heart was still beating. He placed it in a makeshift nest, and sheltered it high in a tree in the backyard. He brought it bits of mashed food every day until it gradually recovered its strength. And after four days, it flew away."

Marion moves forward, the silver streaks in her dark hair glinting in the sun. With shaking hands, she smooths her papers, eyes lowered. "A mother cannot possibly put into words the devastation of losing a child," she says, her voice faltering. "My beautiful son, killed in a far-off country, coming home to me in a flag-draped coffin. . . ." She grips the sides of the podium, and her speech gains volume and conviction: "Jeff was a gentle and compassionate soldier. He was guided by a line he had highlighted in Sun Tzu's *The Art of War*: 'In conflict the less needed the better.' Before he left for Afghanistan, Jeff helped me understand the importance of this mission. He stressed that they were more than a battle group, that it is a humanitarian effort. I was initially opposed to sending our troops there, but I'm proud of my son's dedication to improving the lives of Afghans and making the world a safer place for us all." She concludes with a reference to the farewell letter she sent him: *Jeff— for all that you are, and all that you have accomplished—you are my monument.*

I approach the podium and gaze into all the tear-stained faces. Just off to the right, I catch a glimpse of Gabriel in his navy polo shirt, standing alone on the edge of the crowd, six feet tall and robust for his thirteen years. His shoulders heave, tears roll down his cheeks. Up until now, he has guarded his grief. But the dam has finally burst, washing him into a different world. *Childhood is the kingdom where nobody dies. Nobody that matters, that is.* I take a deep breath, and deliver my words into the listening hearts, into the wind that ferries them over the wave-crested sea. "Like mythical heroes before him," I say in closing, "Jeff inspires each of us to take the journey inside ourselves—to heed our own heart's calling, to face our deepest fears, to give ourselves to some higher end."

Sylvie steps up next, black-rimmed sunglasses shading her eyes. A car swishes by on the road below. A light breeze riffles the flags. "Jeff . . . I can't believe I am standing here today, trying to find the words to describe how I'm feeling," she says, surveying the empty sky. "I miss you so much already. My heart is broken in a million pieces. But I promise you—I'll do my best to pick up one piece up at a time, for the rest of my life. I know I need to be strong for our son, and I promise you, I will find that strength. . . . No words will ever be enough, but I will fill our lives with our stories and memories. Baby, you will always be our Hero . . . my soulmate. And as we always said, instead of goodbye: *until the next time.*

"Now I'd like to read something for Ry," she says, glancing over at her son, who has just awakened from a nap in his stroller. Cuddled in the arms of his uncle Aaron, he wears red-and-white shorts, a matching shirt with an All-England crest—the soccer suit his dad bought for him in England just before his deployment. His cheeks flushed from the heat, his dark blue eyes take in all the faces before him. "This is a passage from *The Little Prince,*" Sylvie says, "one of Jeff's favourite books: *In one of the stars I shall be living. In one of them I shall be laughing. And so it will be as if all the stars were laughing when you look at the sky at night . . .You—you alone—will have the stars as no one else has them.*"

Reverend Jane invites people to come up to share words of remembrance. Herbie Francis, Jeff's eighty-two-year-old grandfather, rises unsteadily from his chair in the front row.

With Russ's guiding arm, he totters up to the podium. In his navy blazer, military medals gleaming on the breast pocket, he struggles to find the words and utter them through his tears: "When I talked to my grandson on the phone before he left, I told him that I didn't want him to go to Afghanistan. And I asked him, 'Why do you have to do this?' Jeff said to me, 'You did it, Gramps.' So there was nothing else that I could say."

The funeral director lowers Jeff's burnished mahogany urn into the red Northumberland soil, as Reverend Jane reads

> Earth brings us into life
> and nourishes us
> Earth takes us back again.
> Birth and death are present in every moment.

Captain Scott Lang stands on guard, still in his tan camouflage uniform and combat boots, saluting his friend and comrade—for the last time. The bagpipes' shrill cry pulls all the teary eyes up the hillside to the graves of our McGrath grandparents and Miller great-grandparents where the kilted piper summons Jeff's return.

> I once was lost but now am found,
> Was blind but now I see.

Our family and friends gradually disperse to gather at the Wallace Community Hall for refreshments—platters of lobster sandwiches and chocolaty sweets, pitchers of cold lemonade, pots of tea and coffee——prepared by Aunt Pearl's United Church Women, the Sisters of Mercy in this small town. I linger behind, talking with my cousin Ralph who has lived in this area all his life. "You don't see those around here very often," he says, pointing up into the open sky.

With spanning wings and fanning tail, golden-brown in the sunlight, a hawk gyrates directly overhead. It hovers, turns and returns, glides in ever-widening circles; then tilts its wing, and soars off over the shimmering sea.

X. DESCENT

———

Nothing can console me. You may bring silk
to make skin sigh, dispense yellow roses
in the manner of ripened dignitaries.
You can tell me repeatedly
I am unbearable (and I know this):
still, nothing turns the gold to corn,
nothing is sweet to the tooth crushing in.

Rita Dove, "Demeter Mourning"

July 22. A scorching prairie sun beats down on her shoulders as Sylvie steps up the sidewalk to a white stucco apartment building with a sign, OFFICERS' QUARTERS, over the entrance. She arrived yesterday at CFB Shilo for the regiment's memorial service. This afternoon she has a couple of hours by herself. She walks slowly down the dimly lit hallway of the first floor, seeking the door with the nameplate *Captain J.C. Francis.* Her hand shakes as she attempts to fit the brass key into the lock. The door creaks open. She crosses the threshold and stands, frozen then closes the door and leans back against it, breathing in the stale air. Shadowy light filters through the half-closed blinds into the living room—beige carpet, cream-coloured walls; a brown couch, TV, stereo—just as he left it six months ago, awaiting his return.

She moves into the bedroom. On his desk are keys, a couple of watches, still silently keeping time, slips of paper. Her fingertips trace his small perpendicular handwriting. The books on the crowded shelves—Foucault, martial arts, military history—volumes of titles, thousands of pages, millions of words he digested. She opens the bifold closet door: his khaki fatigues, maroon Airborne T-shirt, dark green dress uniform, mint-green dress shirt. She buries her face in his uniform, tries to inhale a scent of him; runs her hands over the soft wool of its hollow arms. Shivering, she removes her sandals, and climbs in between the navy fleece sheets of his double bed. For two hours, she lies, enfolded in his green-and-blue plaid comforter, crying into his pillow.

Inanna, the Sumerian goddess of light and life, journeyed to the land of death to free her lover Tammuz. At each of the seven gates of hell, a guardian demanded a piece of her clothing or jewellery as the price of entry—

> *her golden crown*
> *her sapphire earrings*
> *her six-pointed ruby necklace*
> *her star-covered cloak*
> *her jewel-studded shoes*
> *her diamond belt*
> *her shimmering silver skirt.*

Shivering and naked, she approached her elder sister Ereshkigal—
goddess of darkness and death—and the seven judges of the
underworld.

In September, Sylvie puts her one-bedroom condo up for sale and begins house-hunting in Toronto, just as she and Jeff planned two months ago. She traipses through many houses—"perfect for a family"—but can't imagine living in any of them. Nothing seems right. This isn't the way it's supposed to be. After weeks of fruitless looking, she begins to wonder if Toronto is the right place for them. *Should we move? Where do we belong? Who will take care of Ry when I go back to work? Where should he go to school?* She needs to talk to Jeff about all of this, all the decisions she'll now have to make on her own. Waking up every morning to this reality feels like a life sentence. *Can I do this? What's the purpose? Jeff, I need your help. Give me a sign.*

———

RUSS RISES AT SIX in the early morning darkness. He makes his coffee, and takes it to the rocking chair across from the large portrait of Jeff on the corner table. For an hour, he sits in silence, rocking and remembering, and bracing himself for the day ahead. He puts on his striped shirt and a pair of beige pants that were Jeff's. He is comforted by cloth against his skin that once touched his son's. He drives Jeff's black VW Golf across the Murray MacKay Bridge to Gottingen Street, and parks behind the concrete office block of Canadian Blood Services. As he takes the elevator up to his fourth floor office, he dons his mask—smiling, level-headed, in control.

He returns home at 5:00 and lounges on the deck with a Guinness. He stares out at the undulating waves, and cries. Darkness descends. In the living room, he lights the seven white candles on the buffet-shrine beneath Jeff's photo, whispering a name as he sets the match to each one: *Captain Jeff Francis, Captain Matthew Dawe, Master Corporal Colin Bason, Corporal Jordan Anderson, Corporal Cole Bartsch, Private Lane Watkins, the Afghan interpreter*—whose name is still unknown, guarded for his family's safety.

Marion wakes in the dim dawn and looks through the picture window onto the fog-bound sea. All the familiar moorings have disappeared. A Sea King helicopter from CFB Shearwater whirrs over the water. *They're looking for the house,* she thinks. *They're bringing him home. It's all been a mistake.* Her jeans and sweatshirt, lying on the chair beside the bed, remind her that she has to get up. She will make it through this day, just this one day. She peers into the bathroom mirror and recoils at the alien face reflected there— puffy eyes, dark circles, furrowed frown lines, greying hair that gets shorter and shorter.

> *After Osiris's death, Isis cut off her hair and wandered the Nile in search of him. When she found his coffin, she threw herself upon it and wailed. A child, passing by, gaped at her disfigured face, and died of fright.*

She doesn't know how she can live without Jeff in this world. She cannot imagine the future without him. She borrows books from the library about grieving the loss of a child: *Lament for a Son; A Broken Heart Still Beats: When Your Child Dies; What Forever Means: After the Death of a Child; When the Bough Breaks* . . . parents telling stories about what she, herself, is enduring. She's not alone. It is possible to survive. The books become her companions—they understand, and relieve her isolation. Her friends are all moving forward with their lives, chatting about their kitchen renovations and visits with their children. But she is walking backwards—to a year ago when the world was still inhabited by her living son.

One sunny spring day, the goddess Demeter and her daughter Persephone were gathering crocuses and violets in a lush meadow. Persephone strayed from her mother to pick a golden narcissus. The earth opened. Pluto, god of the dead, grabbed Persephone and carried her down to his kingdom in the underworld. Hearing her cries, Demeter flew off in search of her daughter. She wandered the earth for nine days and abandoned all her divine functions as earth-mother. The rain stopped. Streams and rivers dried up; crops died; animals grew infertile. The earth became a desert.

When Zeus realized the gods would also lose their share of the earth's gifts, he ordered Pluto to return Persephone to her mother for half of the year. During the other six months, she lived with her husband in the dark underworld. As Demeter mourns the loss of her child during the months of deep fall and winter, the earth becomes a barren, frozen land.

Marion reads, voraciously, books about afterlife communications: *We Don't Die, The Bridge over the River: After
Death Communications of a Young Artist Who Died in World War
One, To Dance with Angels, The Spiritual Lives of Bereaved Parents.*
They affirm her belief that her son lives on—somewhere,
and they set her on a quest to find him. From a list of ac-
credited psychic mediums, she selects a name, the minister of an American spiritualist church. She's a clairvoyant
who attempts to connect with a particular loved one on the
other side, but makes no guarantees about who will "come
in" during the session. Marion makes an appointment for
a one-hour reading over the phone. The week before, she
lights a candle and meditates every day, strives to empty her
mind and see a white light, a blue aura. She invokes Jeff's
spirit, tells him about the date and time, and pleads with
him—*I need to hear from you.*

The scheduled day arrives. She paces the floor all morning until the phone rings at one o'clock. For half an hour,
she listens to the medium describe spiritual energies. But
she knows that Jeff isn't present. She receives no personal
details about him or their relationship. Still, she continues
to wander in the land of death, searching for her child. She
contacts another psychic, certified by the Forever Family
Foundation—"where science and spirituality work hand-in-
hand to bring comfort to the bereaved." This medium claims
she will provide knowledge that your loved one lives on.
From the books she has read, Marion knows that a psychic
medium should be able to reveal intimate details that only
she and Jeff would know about. But during the one-hour

telephone reading, the medium speaks only in generalities. Again, Marion learns nothing.

———

MICA AND AARON move into their newly built cedar home secluded in the hemlocks by the West River, just outside Antigonish on Nova Scotia's north coast. They begin new jobs. Aaron manages his father's company, Steel Mac, a supplier of structural steel products; Mica is an outreach worker with the Women's Resource Centre. It's a fresh start. But Mica dwells in the past, with the family that was and never will be again. Her only sibling and best friend has vanished. Her parents have become different people—sad, despairing, suspended in limbo by the thread of a life-line. Every night when she calls, she hears their thin voices, as if they're talking from some cold distant planet. She feels helpless, not knowing how to bring them back, or how to ease their suffering.

> *Ereshkigal, goddess of darkness and death, and the judges of the underworld fastened their icy eyes on Inanna, turned her into a corpse, and impaled her body from an iron stake.*
>
> *When Inanna hadn't returned after three days, her helper Ninshubur went to Enki, the god of wisdom. Enki dispatched two demons to hell with a flask of the water of life. They sprinkled the water sixty times upon Inanna's decaying corpse, and carried her reviving body back through the seven gates. One by one, the guardians returned her clothing and jewels.*

Inanna was restored to the world. But she couldn't completely shake the shades of the dead, the bogies and harpies of hell that clung to her.

———

IT COMES TO SYLVIE one golden October morning. She awakens after an uncommonly restful sleep, the sun filtering through the yellow leaves of the birches outside her bedroom window. The word and the place shine pellucid in her mind. *Ottawa.* Her parents are there to help care for Ry when she returns to work. She'll be doing three-day rotations with Air Canada, flying out on Tuesday mornings and back on Thursday nights. So she could commute to the Toronto airport with a half-hour flight. She won't have the anxiety of finding the right caregiver. Ry will bask in the love and attention of his Nanny and Papa. He could go to Centre des Petites, the French daycare that she attended and loved. Back to her hometown—a smaller, kid-friendlier city, the place Jeff resided for fifteen years, longer than anywhere else. *Jeff, is this where we should go? Give me a sign.*

She starts viewing houses in the Carleton University area where her parents live. Within a few days, she discovers the ideal three-bedroom house with a spacious basement play area and a large backyard on a cul-de-sac. It's only a five-minute walk from a playground where Ry squeals with glee as she pushes him, back and forth, in the baby swing.

———

FOR MARION AND RUSS, Thanksgiving weekend has always been celebrated at Fanjoy's Point. As well as the family gathering for dinner, it's the weekend for closing up the cottage—draining the pipes, cleaning out the fridge and cupboards, stacking lawn furniture in the garage. Marion goes through the motions of the ritualistic dinner: makes the stuffing, cooks the turkey, mashes the potatoes; infuses the cottage with the same savoury scents of Thanksgivings past. But nothing smells or tastes the same. And she does not feel thankful. She simply feels tired, wants the long day to be over; then she can clear up the dishes and go to bed.

She and Russ have always slept in the glassed-in sun porch that overlooks the lake. But lately, Russ has been sleeping in Jeff's room in the bunkhouse adjoining the garage. He finds it consoling, he says; he feels closer to Jeff out there in his bed, surrounded by his clothes and books, and the board games from Jeff and Mica's childhood. As she drifts off to sleep, Marion hears his muffled crying through the open window, mingled with the rustling leaves and the waves shushing on the rocks.

In a beam of light, Jeff is sitting on the bed beside her. He wears his khaki T-shirt and camouflage fatigues. She strokes his arms, his face and the top of his shaven head. "Jeff, it really is you," she says. "You really are here. I can feel you. I have to go get Dad."

"No," he says, "not now. But I'll be back."

"Do you like it there?" she asks. "Is it a better place?"

"It's not better, but it's a good place," he says. "But I'm worried about Ry . . . about how he'll get along without me. And . . ."

"What else?"

"Oh . . . you guys . . . you're probably going to spoil him." He smiles. "But I have to go now."

"Jeff, can you leave me something so I can show Dad and Mica that you were really here?"

He hands her a small khaki notebook with a padded cloth cover.

"And I want to give you something, so you can show Granny and Clifford that you've been here with me," she says, and stretches her rubbery camouflage Support-Our-Troops bracelet off her wrist.

Like a slow dissolve in a movie, he gradually fades out of sight.

In the half-light of early morning, she wakes, filled with the wonder of her dream visitation: the texture of the fine hair on his arms, the stubble on his face, the bristly growth on his shaven head; the sound of his voice, his shy grin. She grabs her journal and writes down all its vivid detail, so alive in her mind. She gets up, and is about to pull the blankets over to make the bed. Against the white sheet lies the camouflage circle of her Support-Our-Troops bracelet. Her eyes fill up with tears, and she smiles. *Yes, he really was here.*

———

WHEN MARION AND RUSS visit the Wallace Cemetery on October 31, faded red, orange and yellow leaves blanket the gravesite. On top of Jeff's military marker sit two small pumpkins.

As soon as they arrive back home, they phone Sylvie to tell her about the pumpkins that have mysteriously appeared on Jeff's grave. "Who could have left them there?" she asks.

"It seems like a strange thing for someone to bring. Anyone but me that is, or . . ." She laughs, warmed by the thought of this manifestation, and the memory of their first date with pumpkins on this day fourteen years ago.

———

GALE FORCE WINDS blow off the Northumberland Strait, and two-metre breakers pound on the shores of Wallace Bay. A relentless downpour pelts the crowd huddled around the cenotaph on one of the darkest, stormiest Remembrance Days in Wallace's sixty years of services. His green-blue MacDonald tartan kilt buffeted by the wind, his forest-green jacket and Glengarry beret sodden with rain, the bagpiper plays a medley of Gaelic laments: "Mists over the Mountains" and "Going Home," the high-pitched melody rising above the bluster of the storm. Marion and Marilyn lay a poppy-studded wreath for their father, following a tradition of many years. Marion, a silver cross pinned to her dark blue anorak, places another wreath for the first time, for her son, his name inscribed—alone—on a side of the black granite pillar:

JEFFERSON CLIFFORD FRANCIS

1970–2007

AFGHANISTAN

After the service, the family drives the few kilometres to the cemetery. The young piper, Corporal Eric Graham from the West Nova Scotia Highland Regiment, positions himself beside a tall pink granite headstone—his great-grandfather's—just behind Jeff's grave. He stands against the wind and the rain, sounding Jeff's threnody down the yellow-brown hillside and over the wave-churning sea:

> And now this soldier, this Scottish soldier,
> who wandered far away and soldiered far away,
> sees leaves are falling and death is calling
> and he will fade away, in that far land.

Back in Eastern Passage that evening, they cook his special dishes: spicy chicken-kung-pao, traditional shepherd's pie and an airy "Gone with the Wind" birthday cake. Jeff's place is set at the table beside his photo. They raise their Scotch glasses to him, toasting his thirty-seventh birthday with a dram of his favourite Glenlivet.

———

ON NOVEMBER 13, Sylvie takes possession of their new home on Sonata Place. She and Ry wander through unfurnished rooms that echo with their own emptiness. Ry—just turned one year old—crawls along the smooth hardwood floors, an eager explorer. He stops at the stairs and pushes himself up onto his feet. He takes a few wobbly steps, his arms out like wings, then collapses into Sylvie's waiting arms. In the bathroom, they look into the wide mirror, smiling at their reflection. "Da-dee!" Ry says.

"Où?" Sylvie asks.

"Là!" he says, pointing into the glass. Sylvie spins around, a tingling down her spine. An invisible presence hovers in the air.

———

WINTER IN EASTERN PASSAGE is long and cold. Wispy sea smoke drifts like phantoms over the iron-grey waves. For Marion and Russ, the frail light and frozen earth reflect their inner being. It is April that's the cruellest month. The greening grass, bursting bulbs, budding lilacs, nesting robins belie their inner wasteland—where nothing is reborn. They haven't yet returned to the world, have no social contacts but close family and friends. Most people don't understand what they're going through, and dispense platitudes to "be strong," "find closure," or "get on with it"—as if their lives were a road trip, and grief but a brief pit stop along the way. Even worse, some acquaintances avoid asking them how they're doing, fearful of evoking their sadness and tears.

News of more deaths in Afghanistan revives the trauma of those darkest days. And the controversy swirling around the Canadian military's continued involvement in the mission rubs salt into their wounds. "Such a waste of life," they hear people say. "Our Canadian soldiers—pawns of the powerful." On April 29, Marion writes in her journal,

A year ago today I hugged Jeff for the last time.
Just finished reading a letter that Nichola Goddard wrote home
to her parents, with this quotation from Theodore Roosevelt—

It is not the critic who counts, not the man who points out how the strong man stumbles, or where the doer of deeds could have done better. The credit belongs to the man who is actually in the arena, whose face is marred by dust and sweat and blood, who strives valiantly . . . who spends himself for a worthy cause; who, at the best, knows in the end the triumph of high achievement, and who, at the worst, if he fails, at least he fails while daring so greatly, so that his place shall never be with those cold and timid souls who have never known neither victory nor defeat.

It says it all, especially to all those anti-Afghanistan armchair cynics who lack knowledge of what this mission is struggling to accomplish, and have no appreciation of the soldiers' dedication to the mission and to each other.

Marion and Russ find scant Canadian military services in place to support the families of fallen soldiers—no groups or networking with other grieving military families. Sylvie is entitled to a few sessions with a bereavement counsellor. "You're doing fine," she tells Sylvie after their third meeting. "No need to come any longer." Sylvie doesn't know how to respond. *Had she answered all the questions properly?* She doesn't feel fine. The life she thought she was living has disappeared; she's lost in a netherworld, groping about in the dark for a way out. So she contacts the Military Family Resource Centre at CFB Downsview. After a couple of sessions, the counsellor tells her she's doing very well. Again,

Sylvie wonders why it doesn't feel that way. When she moves to Ottawa, she attends a civilian spousal support group, Grieving Families of Ottawa, for eight weeks. But the spouses are older, with adult children; they can't relate to her situation any more than she can identify with theirs.

No support services are available for Mica. The sibling is the person that's overlooked, she comes to realize; the concern is mainly for the parents and the spouse. Mica also derives solace through reading, but few books focus specifically on sibling loss. As executor of Jeff's will, she encounters resistance from the National Student Loan Service Centre in forgiving a small balance remaining on Jeff's student loan. After months of trying to talk with someone besides a call centre operator, a bureaucrat informs her that no one in the federal government has the authority to forgive this loan; there is no legislation in place for this situation. "This isn't about the amount of money," she tells him. "It's the principle. My brother gave his life in service to our country." Firm in her conviction, she contacts the MLA of her riding, Peter Mackay—then Minister of Foreign Affairs—and the loan is soon repealed.

On the first and third Tuesday of every month, Marion and Russ drive to the St. Vincent de Paul Church in Cole Harbour. In a carpeted meeting room, they sit in leather chairs around a table with several other people, all parents who have lost a child. The bereavement counsellor, Vince MacDonald, initiates discussion by reading a poem or a story, or asking someone about their week. But he allows the parents to direct the conversation or to just be silent. On the table in front of each mother and father is a photo of their child, a ceramic heart and a lighted candle. When new people join the group, the members introduce themselves by telling the story of their child's death. Some are newly grieving parents—one young couple has recently lost their ten-month-old baby. Some have been dealing with their loss for many years, such as the father whose thirty-two-year-old daughter committed suicide ten years ago.

They tell their stories openly and honestly. They each inhabit their own territory of grief, but they speak a common language. For Russ, it's a safe place to talk—to remove his armour and expose the wounds just below the surface. Marion mainly listens, and cries. Talking with people who are travelling the same road makes their burden more endurable. They are not alone. And they learn from the long-term travellers that there's no timetable for the journey.

One evening when Marion and Russ are the only parents present, Vince asks her, "So how's it going?"

"It's hell," she says. "Our life is hell. The emptiness is unbearable most of the time."

"Are you getting out much? Seeing other people?"

"No. I have no desire or energy," she says. "Just getting through the day is exhausting."

"It's the emptiness that's so heavy," he says, rising from his chair. "I'll be right back."

In a few minutes he returns, holding a large grey rock in his hands. "Your grief is like this stone," he says, "weighing you down as you carry it around all day. When you go out, you can make a decision to set it aside; leave it by the door, then pick it up again when you get home."

The group teaches them such strategies for making their sorrow livable. And as they focus on ways of continuing their relationship with their lost child, Marion begins to envision. What does she envision? Jeff's garden—a Zen garden on his granny's land by the sea.

Marion digs in the red earth, plants hostas, ferns and ornamental grasses. She and Russ lug flat sandstones up from the beach for pathways, and shovel pea gravel into beds. They rake the pearl-grey pebbles into a pattern of waves, outlined with sea glass—translucent shards of blue, white and green. In the circular plot, they erect granite standing stones; arrange Japanese solar lanterns and pagodas. Marion is most at peace when she's working in the garden. She feels connected to her son, as if she's caring for him, nurturing his spirit, keeping him alive in this ever-growing, ever-changing entity. Near the entrance, they place a stone meditation bench and a bronzed statue of the Buddha. In a nook formed by three spruce trees, they set a chiselled stone marker: *Jeff's Way*.

EPILOGUE

———

What we call the beginning is often the end
And to make an end is to make a beginning
The end is where we start from.

T.S. Eliot, "Little Gidding"

The highway leading to CFB Shilo in southern Manitoba
is like none other in Canada. Yellow ribbons as tall as a man
festoon the weathered grey fence posts and telephone poles
that line the road, mile after mile. They usher us—Marion,
Russ, Mica, Aaron, Sylvie, Ry and me—to the Home Station
of the First Royal Canadian Horse Artillery. We are driving
to the base for the ceremonial dedication of a trig point in
Jeff's name. A fixed survey marker positioned on a hill in the
military training area, a trig point helps soldiers to orient
themselves during field exercises.

The gravel road into the training zone cuts through
fields of reddish-yellow grass and birch trees, amber leaves
quivering against the bluest widest sky imaginable. We drive
in silence, each of us immersed in our separate spheres of
thought. On this sun-drenched September morning, it
feels like the most peaceful place on earth; this place where

soldiers learn to fire weapons and engage in combat, soldiers committing their lives so we can live in this peaceable land. I imagine Jeff directing his LAV along this track, preparing for the mission of his life: leaving his name in a faraway desert, so a young Afghan girl can write hers for the first time. His samurai sword sharpened her pencil, cut the small square of paper that a veiled woman slips into a ballot box in a remote desert polling station; it fanned a quavering flame of democracy—Afghanistan's only hope for deliverance. Jeff and scores of his comrades relinquishing their today for humanity's tomorrow.

I stroke the "Void" tattoo on my forearm—*When your spirit is not in the least clouded, when the clouds of bewilderment clear away.* "Look over there," Russ says, pointing out his window on the other side of the van. Above the margin of white birches, a hawk is circling, riding the wind ever forward along the road, as if it's showing us the way.

We arrive at a hillock, the only rise of land for miles, and clamber over the rough ground, fragrant with juniper and sage. On the other side of the hill, the C Battery troops stand in rows. Folding metal chairs are lined up for us in front of a wooden podium bracketed by the Canadian flag, the blue-red RCHA flag and large speakers.

"Jeff was a somewhat reserved person who didn't like a lot of fuss," says Major Fortin, the battery commander, "but Jeff—I know you're looking down on this ceremony and blushing—please indulge us for a few moments while we talk about you here." Minutes later, the PA system cuts out. We are sitting close enough to hear without the microphone being used, but the sound waves are lost in the open prairie, drifting up and over the ears of the helmeted soldiers positioned behind the speaker.

The base padre, in a flowing black robe, takes the podium. "Holy places can happen whenever an encounter with the divine occurs," he says. "This trig point will be a place of remembrance, a place of honour in our training field. Let it always remind us of the principles Captain Francis stood for, the expertise and compassion he brought to his work as an artillery officer. May this dedication help us to follow his example of leadership and courage throughout our lives."

Our eyes turn to the crown of a grassy hill where two soldiers unveil a two-metre tripod of blue and red steel, a white-lettered sign on top: FRANCIS. "Trig Francis will always remain in this location, serving as a navigational aid," says Major Chris Henderson, Jeff's commanding officer in Afghanistan. "Each time we pass it on exercise or during training, we will be reminded of Jeff's commitment to his comrades and country."

"Take post!" shouts Major Fortin. The soldiers sprint en masse down the firing range to four Howitzers, cannon-like guns. Restless in his stroller, Ry thrusts his legs excitedly. "Kick, kick," he says, thinking these men are surely running out to play soccer. Jeff's G 1-3 FOO party bellows the call for fire. Four gunshots thunder through the still air. After each round of fire all is starkly silent, but for Ry calling out, "Boom, boom . . . Da-dee." A sixteen-gun salute, Jeff's final round of fire.

The Lucky 13 crew invites us to drive back to the base with them, so Russ, Mica, Aaron, Sylvie and I put on the heavy helmets and climb inside the gloomy interior of the LAV. Rolling along the dirt road in windowless confinement, I envision travelling in this steel encasement across a desert, knowing it could explode beneath me at any second. I take a turn standing up through the hatch, the sun and wind on my face, breathing in the austere beauty of the prairie. Beside me, signaller David Fradette stares off into the distance, pensive, perhaps assimilating the strangeness of transporting Jeff's family. Just a short time ago, Jeff sat in the commander's seat of their Lucky 13 LAV, leading them on.

At the luncheon reception back at the base, the men in Jeff's crew—Clay Cochrane, Adam Wierenga, Carlo Lajoie and David Fradette—chuckle about the sound system malfunctioning during the dedication ceremony. "It had Jeff's signature all over it," says Clay, grinning with reminiscence.

"Yeah," Adam says, "so often Jeff's headphones wouldn't work."

"And remember the two-way radio?" Carlo says. "How it was always cutting out while he was using it?"

I ask them how they've been doing since returning from Afghanistan, and they become subdued, look down at their dusty boots. "You're so busy over there that you just carry on," Clay says. "It's later that it sinks in. Arriving back home was bittersweet. I think of Jeff every day." He glances at the Lucky 13 tattoo on his forearm. "I've had to go to counsellors . . . I haven't been myself. Jeff's death and Afghanistan have changed me."

Russ moves up beside me and takes my arm. "There's one other person we must talk to before we leave," he says, steering me towards Major Henderson, Jeff's commanding officer in the July fourth operation. "I need to hear it from the horse's mouth."

"Was Jeff performing his normal role as FOO that day?" Russ asks. "Why was he in that vehicle? I'm asking this because one Halifax newspaper reported that he'd volunteered to help out when a sixth person was needed."

"I heard about that article," Major Henderson says, crossing his arms over his chest. "Let me set it straight. Jeff was doing the job he was paid to do." As he explains about Jeff coming to him the night before, and about the fog, he talks at a rapid-fire pace, like someone fuelled by caffeine—or anxiety. "So that's why Jeff ended up in Matt Dawe's vehicle. It was a total fluke—there happened to be an empty seat."

"One more question," Russ says, eyes watery. "When you opened up the hatch . . . anybody alive?"

The Major shakes his head. "Jeff was the first to be recovered. He was sitting right by the door."

An unassuming mound of earth in the Canadian prairie is sacred ground. Trig Francis shows the way.

———

I SIT DOWN WITH a large white box packed with sympathy cards and letters that Marion and Russ have received. As I peruse them, I'm astounded by the web of relationships woven around Jeff, and the impact of his life and death on people I've never met. One of longest and most reflective letters is from his friend at Carleton University, Joselyn Morley:

Jeff helped me learn that people transcend the boxes that others put them in. He could be different things at the same time, and somehow the different parts still complemented each other. People write that he was a soldier's soldier, but not just a soldier. . . . or he was really smart, but not a snob. The soldiers had to reconcile that part of Jeff that enjoyed the intellectual pursuits, and the intellectuals had to reconcile the part of Jeff that was a great soldier. I find it easier to reconcile all my own parts when I think of him. I can be a pacifist that understands and appreciates the Armed Forces.

I needed to understand why Jeff enlisted, so I did a lot of research about the Canadian military. Then I encouraged my partner, Marty, to enlist. He had college diplomas in computer technology and programming, but had been either under-employed or unemployed for a long time. I'm not sure we would have survived as a couple without Marty joining the army. He's a changed man—confident, challenged, and rewarded for his initiative.

Jeff's search for meaning——ultimately leaving Carleton and joining the Army——reminds me what determination is. Looking for integrity. Looking for honesty. Looking inside like he did.

Another letter is from a woman that neither Jeff nor anyone in our family has ever met——Renee Naimon, regional director for Canadian Blood Services in central Ontario:

Your son gave his life to the fragile dream of peace and for the security of others. His life had this richness of commitment and a huge, yet unknown, effect on others. I am, myself, a product of those brave souls that fight for freedom as my parents survived the holocaust of World War II by being liberated by soldiers like your son. Because of soldiers like him, they were reborn when they settled in Canada. My brother and I owe our own lives to soldiers who assist those in need of protection. Your son's life was large and very important. Without people like him and parents like yourself, who must soldier the pain of loss, our way of life and freedom would not exist.

———

Jeff kept a reading journal while he was a soldier, a black hardcover notebook in which he recorded quotations from books he was reading. Titles such as *Comprehensive Asian Fighting Arts, Gilles Deleuze and the Philosophy of Difference, The End of History and the Last Man, Postmodern War: The New Politics of Conflict.* The last entry in the notebook comes from the German philosopher G.W.F. Hegel, *The Phenomenology of Mind:*

> And it is solely by risking life that freedom is obtained
> . . . the essential nature of self-consciousness is not bare
> existence, is not the merely immediate form in which it
> at first makes its appearance. The individual who has not
> staked his life may, no doubt, be recognized as a person;
> but he has not obtained the truth of this recognition as
> an independent self-consciousness.

He circled this final passage with fluorescent orange marker. Many blank pages follow, pages never to be written on—half of a notebook, half of a life. But the part that was writ, was writ large—in his small, floating script: the examined life, "not bare existence." *Amor fati.*

———

My shore property will belong to all my grandchildren. Wouldn't it be great if you could build a cottage down there? Dreams do come true, Jeffy.

Letter from Granny, February 1998

JULY 4, 2008. When I arrive at the cemetery at noon, everyone is already there—Marilyn, Mica, Aaron, Marion, Russ and Sylvie. Ry—twenty months old now—peeks out from behind his father's black granite headstone. He toddles forth to see the familiar stranger walking up the hill with an armful of pink and purple lupins. I squat to greet him, and a spark of recognition flickers in his blue eyes. Dressed in his red-and-white soccer suit, he now has the soccer ball to go with it. He practises his kicks and throws as we gather around Jeff's stone. Placed three days ago, on Canada Day, it's etched with laser photos of Jeff—some in Afghanistan; one with his newborn son, adjacent to the epitaph

FOR YOUR TOMORROW

His feathery brown hair damp with sweat, Ry can sit only long enough for quick sips of cold lemonade. "Tu as très chaud," I say, holding the plastic cup up to his lips. "Veux-tu nager? On va à Malagash pour nager dans la mer?

"Oui," he nods, smiling, then runs over to his Gramps who is holding a bunch of red and white helium balloons tied with red and white ribbons.

Russ hands each of us one red and one white balloon. "At this time—two o'clock in the afternoon—one year ago," he says with tear-filled eyes, "we learned about Jeff's death. I miss him more than I can say . . . my heart aches for him every day. These balloons are for Jeff and his five comrades. Let's release them into the air."

As the balloons drift up, Ry cries out and clutches his ribbons. "It's okay," his gran says, kneeling beside him, "they're going up to Daddy." He glances over to his father's stone, then looks back up into the sky. He opens his hand, and watches his balloons float up, higher and higher—red and white specks receding into pale blue space.

"Look at the sun," Russ says. A rainbow encircles it. Not a sundog, the white ring that signals inclement weather, but a halo of pastel hues. We stand mesmerized, gazing at the rainbow-circled sun.

The soul moves in circles, said Plotinus, *hovering, returning, and renewing.*

I feel a tug on my skirt. Ry peers up at me with imploring eyes. "Nage?"

"Mais oui," I say, smiling. "On va à Malagash maintenant."

We park in front of a sandy-brown cottage with a red A-shaped roof, tucked in the salt-water maple and spruce trees—"Alma–Cliff Cottage" on the sign above the door. It remains a work in progress on the inside—rafters, two-by-four studs, pressboard walls, electrical wiring still exposed. But it feels homey and comfortable, furnished with our grandparents' wooden drop-leaf table, our uncle's hand-made pine chairs, Mom's and Jeff's linens, kitchen appliances, dishes, cutlery, cooking utensils. Colourful rugs cover the painted cement floor. A picture window looks out upon the sea.

It's our first family gathering at the Alma–Cliff. Ry, the fifth generation on this ancestral land, scampers about, checking out this strange house with curtain walls. From the screened-in porch, he stares out at the seagulls screech-ing over the Strait. We eat warm biscuits topped with juicy strawberries and whipped cream. Then Ry and I don our bathing suits; his is a navy blue UV suit with yellow flames streaking up the sides.

I take his soft hand in mine, and we step down the sandstone path through Jeff's Way, past the ferns, varie-gated hostas and evergreen shrubs, past the horseshoe pits, through the feathery grass. His small sandalled feet stumble on the rocky bank, so I carry him down to the shore. Long-legged sandpipers skitter and squeak, *peet-weet, peet-weet,* heads bobbing into the foam. His toes touch the cool water, and he flinches. But he's soon entranced by this new world of tidal pools—scuttling crabs, iridescent mussel shells, purple starfish, slimy lime-green sea grass draping the boul-ders. He digs in the wet sand with a clamshell and mounds it over the barnacled rocks. I lie down beside him and paddle my feet, gently splashing water over his face. He licks his lips, tastes its saltiness and smiles uncertainly.

I sling him onto my hip, and we wade into the sea. At low tide we can walk out a long way, see through the clear brine, down to the rippled sandbar of the ocean floor. Tiny hermit crabs scurry. Burgundy blobs of jellyfish drift, trailing wispy hair-like tentacles. Yellow-brown strands of seaweed float in the sun-dappled water. We stop and turn around to look back. We are far from the shore where his grandparents stand, waving. Ry gazes at them for several seconds, then turns back and points out to the infinite blue sea and merging sky. "Go!" he says.

And so we go, headlong into the waves.

———

The opening quotation from the foreword to *Outside the Wire: The War in Afghanistan in the Words of Its Participants,* eds. Kevin Patterson and Jane Warren, Random House Canada, by Roméo Dallaire © 2007. Reprinted by permission of Westwood Creative Artists Ltd.

PROLOGUE

The epigraph is from *American Pastoral*, copyright © 1997 by Philip Roth. Used by permission of Houghton Mifflin Harcourt Publishing Company. All rights reserved.

The quotation "We are a spark beleaguered by darkness . . ." is from Earle Birney's poem "Vancouver Lights" in *Fall by Fury,* McClelland & Stewart, 1978.

The Little Prince, Antoine de Saint Exupéry, translated by Katherine Woods, Harcourt Brace, 1971.

Joseph Campbell quotations are from *The Hero with a Thousand Faces,* Princeton University Press, 1949; and *The Power of Myth,* Doubleday, 1988.

"Amor fati" reference is from *Creating a Life: Finding Your Individual Path,* by James Hollis, Inner City Books, 2001.

CHAPTER 1: BIRTH

Katherine G. Sutherland, from her essay "Land of their Graves" in *Response to Death: The Literary Work of Mourning,* ed. Christian Riegel, University of Alberta Press, 2005. Reprinted with permission.

Saint Martin's story appears in *The Catholic Encyclopedia.* www.newadvent.org.

The Joseph Campbell quotation is from *The Hero with a Thousand Faces,* Princeton University Press, 1949.

The Rudolf Steiner quotation is from a lecture cited without reference by Elisabeth Vreede in *Anthroposophy and Astrology: The Astronomical Letters of Elisabeth Vreede,* Steiner Books, 2001.

The Goethe quotation is from *Conception, Birth & Early Childhood,* by Norbert Glas, Steiner Books, 1983.

The information and quotations about Mars and Scorpio come from *The Penguin Dictionary of Symbols,* by Jean Chevalier and Alain Gheerbrant, translated by John Buchanan-Brown, Penguin, 1969.

The John Prebble quotation is from *The Highland Clearances,* Penguin, 1963.

Angus Sutherland's story appears in *The Rise and Decline of the Community of Earltown: 1813-1970,* by G.R. Sutherland, Colchester Historical Museum, 1980.

The Catharine Parr Traill quotation is from *The Backwoods of Canada,* McClelland & Stewart, 1966.

The Samuel Johnson quotation is in *How Scots Invented the Modern World*, by Arthur Herman, Crown, 2001.

James Hillman, *A Terrible Love of War,* Penguin, 2004.

St. Christopher's story is from *The Catholic Encyclopaedia*. www.newadvent.org.

The story of Thetis and Achilles appears in *Mythology: Timeless Tales of Gods and Heroes*, by Edith Hamilton, Grand Central Publishing, 1969.

Leonard Cohen's "Closing Time," from the CD *The Future,* Sony, 1992.

Jung quotation from *Children's Dreams,* Princeton University Press, 2008.

Joseph Campbell quotation from *The Power of Myth,* Doubleday, 1988.

Rita Dove quotation from her poem "Mother Love," in *Mother Love: Poems,* Norton, 1996.

CHAPTER 2: CHILD OF DESTINY

David Adams Leeming, *Mythology: The Voyage of the Hero,* Oxford, 1998. Reprinted with permission of Oxford University Press, Inc.

Carlos Castaneda, *The Teachings of Don Juan: A Yaqui Way of Knowledge,* Washington Square Press, 1996.

"I am a part of all that I have met" is from Tennyson's poem "Ulysses," *The Norton Anthology of English Literature*, 7th ed. Norton, 2001.

"[T]hrough the unknown, remembered gate" is from T.S. Eliot's poem "Little Gidding," *The Norton Anthology of English Literature,* 7th ed., Norton, 2001.

CHAPTER 3: CROSSROADS

James Hollis, *Creating a Life: Finding Your Individual Path,* Inner City Books, 2001. Reprinted with permission.

CHAPTER 4: THE VOID

Miyamoto Musashi, *A Book of Five Rings,* translated by Thomas Cleary, Shambhala, 2000.

Chögyam Trungpa, *Shambhala: The Sacred Path of the Warrior,* Shambhala, 2007.

James Hollis, from *Creating a Life: Finding Your Individual Path,* Inner City Books, 2001.

Salary figures for Canadian Forces members and civilian workers are from a Statistics Canada report by Jungee Park, "A Profile of the Canadian Forces" in *Perspectives* (July 2008).

The phrase "changed, changed utterly" is from W.B. Yeats's poem "Easter 1916," *The Norton Anthology of English Literature,* 7th ed., Norton, 2001.

Van Morrison's "The Philosopher's Stone" is from the CD *The Philosopher's Stone,* Polydor, 1998.

Joseph Campbell, *The Power of Myth*, Doubleday, 1988.

"It is easier not to take the journey . . . but then life can dry up" is from *The Power of Myth.*

"'Hope' is the thing with feathers," Emily Dickinson, *Complete Poems of Emily Dickinson,* ed. Thomas H. Johnson, Back Bay Books, 1976.

"[T]o strive, to seek, to find, and not to yield" is from Tennyson's poem "Ulysses," *The Norton Anthology of English Literature,* 7th ed., Norton, 2001.

Nichola Goddard's letter is in *Outside the Wire: The War in Afghanistan in the Words of Its Participants,* ed. Kevin Patterson and Jane Warren, Random House, 2007.

CHAPTER 5: GOODBYE

Excerpt from *Heroes: The Champions of Our Literary Imaginations,* copyright 2007, by Bruce Meyer, published by HarperCollins Publishers Ltd. All rights reserved.

Timothy Findley, *The Wars,* Penguin, 1977.

CHAPTER 6: AFGHANISTAN

Joseph Campbell, *The Power of Myth,* Doubleday, 1988. Reprinted with permission.

"Fear no more the heat 'o the sun . . ." is a quotation from Shakespeare's play *Cymbeline* in *William Shakespeare: The Complete Works,* ed. Alfred Harbage, Penguin, 1969.

The Aztecs' "the house of the sun" is from *The Codex Mendoza,* Vol. 1., by Frances F. Berden and Patricia Rieff Anawalt, University of California Press, 1991.

CHAPTER 7: ASCENSION

"The Flight of Quetzalcoatl" is from *Technicians of the Sacred: A Range of Poetries from Africa, America, Asia, and Oceania,* 2nd ed., Jerome Rothenberg, University of California Press, 1985. Reprinted with permission.

CHAPTER 8: TEARS

Archibald Macleish, "Ars Poetica," *Archibald MacLeish: Collected Poems 1917-82,* Houghton Mifflin, 1985. Copyright © 1985 by The Estate of Archibald MacLeish. Reprinted by permission of Houghton Harcourt Publishing Company. All rights reserved.

The quotation "Home they brought her warrior dead . . ." is from Tennyson's poem "The Princess," in *Tennyson: Poems,* Knopf, 2004.

The story of Isis comes from James Frazer's *The New Golden Bough,* S.G. Phillips, 1959.

Niobe's story appears in *Bulfinch's Mythology: The Age of Fable*, by Robert Graves, Doubleday, 1968.

CHAPTER 9: FIFTY BRIDGES

Chase Twichell, "Saint Animal," *The Snow Watcher Poems,* Ontario Review Press, 1998. Reprinted with permission.

"The dove is never free" is from Leonard Cohen's song "Anthem" on the CD *The Future,* Sony, 1992.

Sun Tzu, *The Art of War,* Dover, 2002.

"Childhood is the kingdom where nobody dies . . ." is from Edna St. Vincent Millay's poem "Childhood Is the Kingdom Where Nobody Dies," *The Norton Anthology of Literature by Women,* eds. Sandra Gilbert and Susan Gubar, Norton, 1985.

Reverend Jane's verse is from *Peace in Every Step,* by Thich Nhat Hanh, Bantam, 1992.

CHAPTER 10: DESCENT

Rita Dove's poem "Demeter Mourning" is in *Mother Love: Poems,* Norton, 1996. Copyright 1995 by Rita Dove. Used by permission of W.W. Norton and Company, Inc.

Inanna's story is from *Sumerian Mythology* by S.N. Kramer, Harper Torchbooks, 1961; and *Myths of the Female Divine Goddess*, by David Leeming and Jake Page, Oxford, 1994.

The stories of Isis and Demeter come from *The New Golden Bough* by James Frazer, S.G. Phillips, 1959.

The Theodore Roosevelt quotation is in Nichola Goddard's letter in *Outside the Wire: The War in Afghanistan in the Words of Its Participants,* eds. Kevin Patterson and Jane Warren, Random House Canada, 2007.

EPILOGUE

T.S. Eliot, "Little Gidding," *Four Quartets,* Faber and Faber, 1942. Reprinted with permission of Faber and Faber Ltd.

G.W.F. Hegel, *The Phenomenology of Mind,* translated by J.B. Baillie, Dover Publications, 2003.

ACKNOWLEDGEMENTS

I am deeply indebted to many people for their contribution, advice and support during the writing of this book: my friend Mary Ellen Holland, who encouraged me to write it and bolstered me every step of the journey; Jeff's comrades—Scott Lang, Clay Cochrane, Sean Connors, Jason Francis, Craig Ethelston, Stephen Ker, Chris Henderson, Tim Haveman—who told their stories about Jeff as a soldier, his final mission and the aftermath of his death; Joselyn Morley, Pauline Rankin and Alan Hunt, who relayed their memories of Jeff during his decade at Carleton University.

Lee Windsor, David Charters and Brent Wilson's book, *Kandahar Tour: The Turning Point in Canada's Afghan Mission*, was an indispensable source of information on Task Force 1-07's training and its operations in Kandahar province.

I am grateful to Karen Connelly, my mentor at the Humber School of Creative Writing, for her invaluable guidance; to my editor, Craig Pyette, for his unfailingly sound, insightful editorial suggestions; to Doris Cowan for her astute copy editing; and to Denise Bukowski, my literary agent par excellence.

I wish to thank Okanagan College for granting me financial assistance and release time to work on this project, as well as my English Department colleagues for their steadfast encouragement, especially Frances Greenslade, John Lent, Alix Hawley and Craig McLuckie.

Finally, this book could not have been written without the involvement and loving support of my family: my son, Damian, who drove me around the Scottish Highlands; Marion, Russ, Mica, Sylvie and Marilyn—who delved into their deep wells of memory and allowed me to be the *seannachie*.

MELANIE MURRAY grew up in the military town of Oromocto, New Brunswick, during the 1960s while her father was a soldier at CFB Gagetown. She has been living in Kelowna, British Columbia, since 1987, teaching English at Okanagan College and raising her two sons, Damian and Gabriel. Captain Jeff Francis is her nephew. *For Your Tomorrow* is her first book.

www.melaniemurray.ca

A NOTE ABOUT THE TYPE

For Your Tomorrow has been set in Perpetua, a typeface designed by the English artist Eric Gill, and cut by the Monotype Corporation between 1928 and 1930. Perpetua is a face of original design, without historical antecedents. The shapes of the roman characters are derived from the techniques of stonecutting. Originally intended as a book face, Perpetua is unique amongst its peers in that its larger display characters retain the elegance and form so characteristic of its book sizes.

Appropriate to its heritage, Perpetua's titling caps are often used to inscribe headstones and rememberance monuments.

BOOK DESIGN BY CS RICHARDSON